THE·APPIAN·WAY

THE·APPIAN·WAY
GHOST·ROAD,
QUEEN·OF·ROADS

ROBERT·A·KASTER

University of Chicago Press
Chicago and London

Robert A. Kaster, professor of classics and Kennedy Foundation Professor of Latin at Princeton University, has taught and written mainly in the areas of Roman rhetoric, the history of education, and Roman ethics. His books include *Guardians of Language: The Grammarian and Society in Late Antiquity* (Berkeley: University of California Press, 1988), *Emotion, Restraint, and Community in Ancient Rome* (Oxford: Oxford University Press, 2005), and several critical editions and translations, including *Seneca: Anger, Mercy, Revenge* (with Martha C. Nussbaum) in the University of Chicago Press's Complete Works of Seneca series (2010).

The University of Chicago Press, Chicago 60637
The University of Chicago Press, Ltd., London
© 2012 by The University of Chicago
All rights reserved. Published 2012.
Printed in the United States of America

21 20 19 18 17 16 15 14 13 12   1 2 3 4 5

ISBN-13: 978-0-226-42571-9(cloth)
ISBN-10: 0-226-42571-1 (cloth)

Library of Congress Cataloging-in-Publication Data

Kaster, Robert A.
    The Appian Way : ghost road, queen of roads / Robert A. Kaster.
        p. cm. — (Culture trails)
    ISBN-13: 978-0-226-42571-9 (cloth : alkaline paper)
    ISBN-10: 0-226-42571-1 (cloth : alkaline paper) 1. Appian Way (Italy) I. Title. II. Series: Culture trails.
    DG29.A6K37 2012
    937′.7—dc23

2011032769

♾ This paper meets the requirements of ANSI/NISO Z39.48–1992 (Permanence of Paper).

For Laura

CONTENTS

PREFACE

Billy Pilgrim says that the Universe does not look like a lot of bright little dots to the creatures from Tralfamadore. The creatures can see where each star has been and where it is going, so that the heavens are filled with rarefied, luminous spaghetti. And Tralfamadorians don't see human beings as two-legged creatures, either. They see them as great millipedes—"with babies' legs at one end and old people's legs at the other," says Billy Pilgrim.

—KURT VONNEGUT, JR., *Slaughterhouse-Five*
(on seeing in four dimensions)

The Roman poet Statius called the via Appia *regina viarum*, "the Queen of Roads," late in the first century CE, when the title—despite sounding like chamber-of-commerce puffery—could make a decent claim to the truth. As for the other phrase in my subtitle, "Ghost Road," that one came to me one afternoon as my wife and I walked along the road's modern traces. For to travel the Appia today is to step in the tracks of countless ghosts.

No road in Europe has been so heavily traveled, by so many different people, with so many different aims, over so many generations. Standing in one spot, eyes shut, a traveler does not need much imagination to feel the ghosts brush by. A Roman soldier first, as the power of his city forced its way south and laid its weight upon the other tribes of the peninsula, who sometimes managed to push back. Then a craftsman, tradesman, or small farmer bringing his goods to one of the towns—Minturnae or Aeclanum or Venusia—that were the links in the civil life of a great empire. Now more soldiers, in wave after wave, first sweeping up from the south with the power of Constantinople at their backs, then down from the north—first the Lombards, later the Normans (and many others)—to settle in the strongholds of Beneventum, Melfi, and countless other hill towns where castles still punctuate the ridges. Pious travelers came this way, too, journeying to Jerusalem with stage-by-stage directions that we can still follow. Then closer to our own day, scholars and statesmen, the one lot intent on reclaiming ancient bits of the road in the eighteenth and nineteenth centuries (and on down to the present day), the other following the road on the way to a unified Italy. If we could take in the Appia with the eyes of Vonnegut's Tralfamadorians, we would see a millipede shod at one end in the sandals of Appius Claudius Caecus—who conceived the road and gave it his name— and in the shoes of Garibaldi's horse near the other end.

It's a sense of this cultural richness that I've tried to convey in these essays, by telling the story of the road from my own perspective, that of a very imperfectly savvy traveler. Though my profession as a classicist allowed me to begin traveling along the Appia with a few advantages—chiefly, a fair knowledge of Latin and a reasonable sense of Roman history—the pockets of my ignorance were far deeper and more numerous. Traveling the Appia was an intense education, and a goad to learn more: the intensity and the excitement of learning are among the forces that drive this book.

Thanks by the carload are owed on several fronts. Susan Bielstein, editor of the Culture Trails series at the University of Chicago Press, suggested that I might contribute to the series, was instantly receptive when I proposed the Appia, and lavished her attention on the initial draft; the Press's Anthony Burton has been helpful in ways technical and nontechnical alike; two readers helped me see where some improvements could be made; and Carol Saller was the perfect copyeditor. Of the two chances I've had to travel the route, the first and longer came during a sabbatical year provided by Princeton University and the University's Humanities Council, which appointed me an Old Dominion Professor in 2008–2009; both trips were partly funded by the Dean of the Faculty and by the Magie Fund in Princeton's Department of Classics, which has been repeatedly generous in its support of my work. Then there are the friendly critics who have done their best to keep me from appearing foolish in print: Yelena Baraz, Ted Champlin, Janet Downie, Elaine Fantham, Denis Feeney, Andrew Feldherr, Harriet Flower, Laura Kaster, Joshua Katz, Chris Kraus, Nino Luraghi, Adrienne Mayor, Brent Shaw, Chris Stray, Stefan Vranka, and Leah Whittington. If they have not wholly succeeded, the fault as always is entirely mine.

This is the second and a half book that I've dedicated to my wife, Laura. (She shared with my parents the dedication of my first: uncertain back then that I'd ever write another, I thought I'd better touch all the bases while I had the chance.) For forty-odd years she has nurtured everything I've written and cast a keen critical eye over much of it, but she has never before been the close collaborator that she was in the travels from which this little book has emerged. Without her, my experience of the Appia would have been thinner and poorer in more ways than I can count; without her, my life would be thinner and poorer in more ways than I can imagine.

I
QUEEN·OF·ROADS
Rome and the Appian Way

What the hell are we doing here?

The question formed in my mind as the umpteenth car whipped past, inches from my right kneecap, leaving a trail of noxious fumes in its wake. We were making our way back to the city walls of Rome, my wife and I, on a stretch of the ancient Appian Way, between the catacombs of San Sebastiano and San Callisto, where Christians of ancient Rome buried their dead. With about two miles to go, we walked single file, huddling against the walls that hemmed in the left side of the Appia, and flinching as each car went by.

We had begun the day at the spot where the Appia once began, the porta Capena, the main gate in the southeast quadrant of Rome's most ancient walls. The walls—the Servian walls, according to legend built by king Servius Tullius in the mid-sixth century BCE—are long gone, and with them the gate. For that matter, the Appia is gone there too, replaced by one of the busiest intersections in modern Rome, where traffic streams to and from the Colosseum or past the broad expanse of the Circus Maximus. But a plaque on a clump of ancient brick ruins marks the *inizio della via Appia*, and it's not hard to follow the path from there, across several lanes of traffic, that the road must have traced, to the point where it split off from the via Latina, which followed a more easterly course out to the hills where Roman grandees had their villas. About a half mile from that point, at the end of a gently rising grade, another gate—the ancient porta Appia, now the porta San Sebastiano—is set in another wall, the

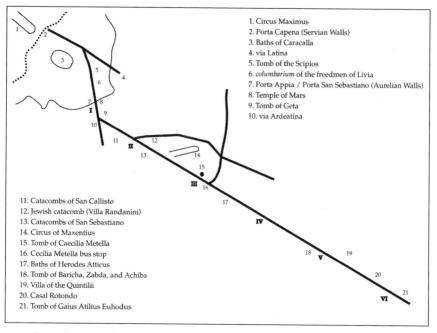

1. Circus Maximus
2. Porta Capena (Servian Walls)
3. Baths of Caracalla
4. via Latina
5. Tomb of the Scipios
6. *columbarium* of the freedmen of Livia
7. Porta Appia / Porta San Sebastiano (Aurelian Walls)
8. Temple of Mars
9. Tomb of Geta
10. via Ardeatina

11. Catacombs of San Callisto
12. Jewish catacomb (Villa Randanini)
13. Catacombs of San Sebastiano
14. Circus of Maxentius
15. Tomb of Caecilia Metella
16. Cecilia Metella bus stop
17. Baths of Herodes Atticus
18. Tomb of Baricha, Zabda, and Achiba
19. Villa of the Quintilii
20. Casal Rotondo
21. Tomb of Gaius Atilius Euhodus

Figure 1. Via Appia, miles 1 to 6

Aurelian, that is many lifetimes younger than the Servian but nonetheless eighteen centuries old today, and here still intact.

Just beyond the porta San Sebastiano stood the first of hundreds of inscribed milestones:* a replica stands there today, roughly marking the spot where the modern archeological "park" begins. The scare quotes are well earned. For perhaps half a mile, from the milestone to the gate of the San Callisto catacombs, as the Appia descends to the bed of a small stream (the Almo), then arcs left to start back uphill, the road is merely ugly: after a tawdry commercial strip (a car dealership, an auto repair shop, storefronts), businesses are replaced by private homes and eight-to-ten-foot-high walls that form a

---

*A milestone (*miliarium*) marked the end of a Roman mile, which was just over nine-tenths as long as our statute mile. In the text, "mile" generally refers to the latter, save with reference to milestones or when expressly called a "Roman mile."

blind, virtually unbroken barrier on both sides of the road. The next stretch, from the San Callisto gate to the San Sebastiano catacombs, is both ugly and terrifying. The road is still hemmed in by the high walls, but now anything like an adequate walkway is gone: a narrow pedestrian strip is distinguished from the driving surface by no more than a painted white line, which drivers feel no compulsion to observe as they gun their engines going in both directions, here and there producing three lanes of traffic (*of course* they have to pass each other) in a space that cannot be more than thirty feet wide wall to wall. So the question: what the hell were we doing there?

The literal answer was simple enough. Though teaching the language and literature of ancient Rome has been my life, I had spent little time in Italy, and virtually none in Rome itself, since the summer of 1973, when I endured several sweltering weeks in the Vatican Library as a graduate student doing research for my dissertation. That had not been a happy time: Laura, my wife, had just finished law school back home in Boston and was studying for the bar exam, and we were both lonely in our separate routines. But that was then. Now it was the spring of a sabbatical year, and we were carefree in Italy for a month, half of it to be spent traveling the Appian Way.

That was our mission: to explore the Appia for all it was worth. Our plan: to begin and end in the capital, first tramping over the nine miles of roadway that extend from the city, then changing perspective by picking up from where the Appia ended, at Brindisi (ancient Brundisium)* in the heel of Italy, and working our way back by car to Rome. The first stage would get the feel of the road under our feet and remembrances of Roman power in our imaginations. The second would take us through parts of Italy where we had never traveled and layers of Italian culture we had never seen.

We arrived in Rome on the Parilia—April 21, the city's birthday, with 2,762 candles lit on the imaginary cake—and immediately got

---

*In this essay I use the ancient names of cities when recounting ancient history, and the modern names otherwise. Both forms of the name are found on the map.

Figure 2. Via Appia, mile 2

lucky, in a couple of ways. First, we discovered that we had scheduled our trip so that the first week coincided with the *settimana della cultura*—"Culture Week," a national explosion of pride in Italy's heritage, when special exhibitions and performances are laid on in towns and cities from the Alps to Calabria, and all the museums and archaeological sites are open free of charge. Second, and better still, I made a phone call.

After getting to the hotel we had booked at the foot of the Spanish Steps, we decided to deal with the jet lag as we usually do, by keeping on keeping on until we dropped. I fished out the phone number of Marina Piranomonte, the friend of a friend and a senior member of the ministry in charge of the archaeological sites in Rome. We had arranged that I would call when we arrived. Now seemed as good a time as any, and Marina in fact had space on her calendar to see us. So we walked the half hour or so it takes to get from the Spanish Steps to the Roman Forum, where we were immersed right away in the consequences of Culture Week.

The place was alive with people, cascading through the entrances and flowing down the slope that sets the ancient site apart from the grade of the modern city. Ancient columns rose among the ruins, watching impassively as the human stream flowed past, and within the stream small patterns emerged. Knots of adults gathered here and there on the old paving stones, listening to their guides, while sinuous lines of schoolchildren threaded among them, their teachers leading them two by two. The morning had turned warm and hazy by the time we walked the length of the Forum along the Sacred Way, past the remains of buildings that had stood for up to sixteen hundred years before serving as quarries in the Renaissance. To the left, a temple dedicated in the second century CE to a deified couple, the emperor Antoninus Pius and his wife, Faustina, had surrendered large chunks of itself when the Lateran Palace, the residence of the popes, was rebuilt after a fire in the 1360s. Two hundred years later, a temple on the right, raised to the deified Julius Caesar in the first century BCE, had given up still more of itself for the sake of St. Peter's. Just beyond these remains we climbed a short rise and reached the Forum's eastern end, where the Arch of Titus depicts the sack of Jerusalem in 70 CE and the ruins of the Temple of Venus and Roma have been repurposed to house the church of Santa Francesca Romana and the archaeological ministry. There we presented ourselves.

Marina greeted us warmly, a tall, vivid figure draped in a black cape, her lavender eyeshadow matching her lipstick. (Purple, we discovered, was *the* color of the season.) After some rapid introductions to her colleagues and staff, she swept us through the ministry, through the remains of the ancient sanctuary of Roma with its marble floor and porphyry columns, and out onto a terrace—once the temple's grand entryway—that faces the Colosseum, a hundred yards away. Not bad digs, I thought, feeling a stab of the typical academic's office-envy. Next Marina swept us back into a conference room, where she proceeded to shower us with books about Rome and the Appian Way and with questions about our trip: Where were we going first? How had we made our plans? And why were we doing what we were doing? Her intense interest made plain that what I'd taken to be a courtesy call was turning into something else when suddenly Marina announced, "OK, now we go for a drive."

Drive?

First stop: the Baths of Caracalla, the immense complex built early in the third century CE near the start of the Appia. The Baths draw far fewer visitors today than, say, the Colosseum—but if you want to fill your imagination with the grandeur of an empire at its height, this is much the better place to contemplate. With an Olympic-sized swimming pool, exercise rooms, and halls for cold and hot plunges, the place could accommodate up to ten thousand bathers, providing separate but equal facilities for the sexes. It continued to function as spa, art gallery, and major social center into the sixth century; it also happens to be among the sites Marina oversees, and the subject of one of her books. Then, back in the car, around the corner, and speeding past the tomb of the Scipios on the Appian Way, where six generations of one of Rome's greatest aristocratic families were buried: its members included Scipio Africanus, who defeated Hannibal and saved Rome, and his grandson, Scipio Aemilianus Africanus, who destroyed Carthage street by street and stone by stone fifty-odd years later.

By this point I had shaken off the dazed confusion of jet lag and was far along into being seriously thrilled. Here we were on the road I had come to explore. We pulled through the porta San Sebastiano and into the archaeological park, following the path as it climbed past the catacombs, toward the level stretch that begins about three miles out. There long patches of the original road begin to appear, the irregular blocks of basalt, a foot or more in diameter, emerging from the earth in waves that test a car's suspension, making it pitch and roll like a skiff in a swell. I breathed in the spring air and took in the sights, as Marina pointed out this or that ancient monument, and this or that modern estate that abutted the road. I was blissed out, and utterly, happily oblivious of being the sort of vehicular intruder I'd be cursing as a pedestrian four days later.

So there we were, making our first acquaintance with the Appian Way. But why *there*, in particular? Why—as Marina had put it—were we doing what we were doing? What was the allure of the Appia that had drawn us to it?

Some parts of the answer are obvious and lend themselves to superlatives. The Appian Way was, after all, the *regina viarum*, "queen of roads": so said the poet Statius, who would have used the road numberless times as he shuttled between Rome and his birthplace, Naples. As the first great road of Europe, the Appia in essence defined what a fully built road should be, and it remained for centuries a model of the engineering that was among the Romans' greatest achievements. As the longest of the roads in Italy, when it reached its full extent, it was central to the network that bound together the peninsula, and in time the Empire, and so fostered the formation of a unified culture. Ultimately, the Empire's system of public roads extended an astonishing 75,000 miles: in 2006, the United States had only a bit more than 46,000 miles of interstate highways, serving a population roughly five times as large. As the only road that spanned the length of the peninsula below Rome, the Appia became, mile for Roman mile, the most heavily traveled in the entire system, not just at the height of Rome's Empire but beyond, when it funneled (for example) eager pilgrims on their way to the Holy Land. And, fundamental to our story, it was conceived, near the end of the fourth century BCE, by one man—Appius Claudius Caecus—who is the first Roman we can fairly claim to know as an authentic historical person.

Other reasons why I was drawn to the road are more elusive, and grounded in the imagination. The Appia was frankly a road of power, following the expansion of Rome's influence in Italy and its growth to the greatness of an empire. At the same time, it was, in a particular and important way, a road of death, lined for mile upon mile with the tombs of the great and humble alike, all jostling for space to provide a showplace for their memory. The Appia inspires thoughts of power, death, and remembrance that seem essentially Roman: in a culture that had no belief in a personal afterlife, this was all there was, this time right now, and you had better exert yourself with all the strength and cunning you could muster to establish your name for future generations to remember, and so escape oblivion. Then there are the layers—of time, culture, and human strivings— that the Appia invites the traveler to contemplate as it passes through Lazio (ancient Latium), Campania, Basilicata (Lucania), and Puglia (Apulia), four of the six regions of Italy that lie south of Rome. Here memory of ancient empire recedes into the background, replaced by the monuments of the other conquering peoples—Byzantines, Normans, Swabians, Angevins, Aragonese—who placed their stamp upon the land, as control of southern Italy passed from hand to hand and dynasty to dynasty, century after century. One era rubs up against another, here and there throwing off sparks: "Aha!"

All these parts—complex, multiple, associative—speak to me because my fascination with the past accounts for much of who I am, and all the parts need some space to tell. The many layers of history and culture that the Appia's whole expanse helps to reveal lend themselves better to the next chapter's story, when we will travel the length of the road south of Rome. The other parts, the parts concerned with power, death, and memory, we can begin to think about here, starting with the man who gave the road his name. A vivid character seizing an opportunity, he was the chief reason why this road was built at just the time it was built.

"EACH MAN CRAFTS HIS OWN FORTUNE"

To put Appius Claudius Caecus in perspective we have to step back even further in time to 509 BCE, when the Roman Republic was established.* Unlike the monarchy under which the city had been founded two and a half centuries earlier, the Republic was a community of citizens equal (in principle) before the law, governed by the laws they approved and the magistrates they elected, and keeping track of laws and magistrates was a matter of concern to all of the community's members. So it was under the Republic that the first historical records began to be kept, in the form of the "annals" that the *pontifex maximus*, or supreme priest, compiled each year (*annus* = "year" → *annalēs* = "annals") and posted on a whitened board for the community to read. These were not narratives by any means, but catalogues listing the magistrates elected and other significant events, like military campaigns, scarcities of grain, or portents—the birth of a two-headed calf, for example—that signaled the gods' displeasure and called for expiation.

Not much, perhaps; but at least there were *facts* on record to be used when the Romans themselves began, in the late third and early second century BCE, to write narrative history on the model

---

*From this point the story will shift from one era to another: I use the markers BCE and CE to establish a reference point at the first relevant date each time a shift occurs but as a rule do not repeat them throughout.

of Greeks like Herodotus and Thucydides, constructing plausible stories by combining the annals' data with traditions that individual families handed down. The priestly annals themselves are long gone, and those first histories—largely written by Roman statesmen like Cato the Censor—exist today only as fragments found in later learned sources, including the later historians who drew on them. These are the writers we can now read—above all, Livy on the Latin side (though only a quarter of his huge work survives), or Dionysius of Halicarnassus, Diodorus of Sicily, and Cassius Dio on the Greek (none of their works remotely whole)—as they piece together the slender remains they found and, inevitably, give those remains the slant or coloring or spin suggested by their own times and biases.

In view of all this, then, saying that the man for whom our road is named, Appius Claudius Caecus, emerges from the mists of Rome's poorly documented past as its first historically knowable person is not a modest claim. But it does have the virtue of being true. Relative to some families—the Julii and Sergii, for example—who traced their origins back to the Trojans who came to Italy with Aeneas after the fall of Troy, Appius's family, the Claudii, were newcomers who first migrated to Rome at the end of the sixth century BCE. This is how their story is told by the imperial biographer Suetonius, at the start of his life of the emperor Tiberius, a direct descendent of Appius's son, the first Tiberius Claudius Nero:

> The patrician clan of the Claudii—there was also a plebeian clan, of no less influence and standing—sprung up among the Sabines in the town of Regillum and moved from there to Rome with a large band of dependents soon after the city's founding [i.e., 753] . . . or (as the more reliable version has it) under the leadership of Atta Claudius just about six years after the kings were expelled [i.e., 504*]: there

*The Romans had the custom, odd to the modern eye, of counting inclusively: for example, whereas we refer to the day before yesterday as "two days ago," they said, "it is the third day since . . . ," because they counted today. So the sixth year after 509 is 504, not 503, because 509 itself must be included in the countdown.

they were received among the patricians and given land besides, for their dependents, across the River Anio [northeast of the city].

According to Roman tradition, the Sabines, a rugged people living in the hill-country north of Rome, were the first of the city's neighbors to be blended with its population, through the capture of their marriageable women that Romulus engineered soon after the city's founding ("The Rape of the Sabine Women"). As Suetonius goes on to say, the clan of the Claudii came to be known for "many deeds of exceptional merit on the part of many of its members, but also many actions committed against the common interest." The sorts of actions covered by the latter phrase grew (it was said) out of the extreme arrogance for which the family was known, exemplified by the story of one of its members who led a fleet against the Carthaginians in the First Punic War of the mid-third century. Eager for battle and frustrated by the refusal of the sacred chickens on board to give an auspicious sign by greedily gobbling down their feed, he allegedly tossed them into the sea, saying, "Let them drink, since they don't want to eat!" (He was defeated, of course, and later punished.) But that story should probably be taken with a grain of salt, as should the more general report of the family's extraordinary arrogance—not because they were more likely meek and mild, but because their arrogance was probably no more excessive than the considerable self-regard that the average Roman aristocrat nurtured. In any case, the patrician Claudii came to have much to be proud of, for once they became established in the city they went on to hold more senior political offices under the Republic than most other clans, including the highest office—the consulship—in twelve consecutive generations.

Given the important role that family played at Rome in promoting such success, we might be surprised that any member of the Claudian dynasty was the source of the sentiment that heads this section, though it is in fact the most famous of the sayings attributed to our Appius: *faber est suae quisque fortunae.* The thought that each of us is the *faber*—the craftsman or engineer—of our own fortune, our lot and luck in life, involves notions of individual responsibility and individual freedom, of open-ended achievement and personal potential, that frankly sound more modern American than ancient Roman. But still more surprising and unconventional than his words were the actions he took in shaping his own fortune, when he held his first political office, as censor in the year 312.

The Roman censor's duties had next to nothing to do with what we call "censorship." Instead, a pair of censors was chosen every five years to do two main jobs: to carry out a systematic review of the Roman populace—a census, in fact—that included a survey of every male citizen's financial resources and moral fitness (the latter offers the one point at which the images of ancient and modern censors might overlap); and when that survey was completed, to conduct a ritual purification of the citizen body gathered en masse on the Campus Martius, by leading a pig, a sheep, and an ox around them three times before offering up the animals as sacrificial victims to the gods—scapegoats, in effect, though none of them happened to be an actual goat. In carrying out the census Appius pressed for several measures intended to distribute political influence and authority more evenly throughout the community, beyond the quasi-hereditary oligarchy, centered in the senate, that had come to have a near monopoly on offices and power. It is reported that the measures, with their populist tinge, so outraged his colleague in the censorship that the man resigned.

Now, the depth of Appius's actual populist fervor is unclear, for there are other actions recorded in his career that show him defending patrician privilege against plebeian incursions. It may well be that he was above all a shrewd operator, using his censorship to build a large base of dependents and supporters for greater things to come: a comparison with the career of a later "populist patrician," Julius Caesar, is fair. If that was his plan, it appears to have worked, for he went on to have a political career that lasted another thirty years and boasted no fewer than five senior magistracies, including two terms in the consulship.

But it was two other accomplishments of Appius's censorship that most concern us. Both were public works that he undertook, allegedly without the senate's sanction and at a cost that depleted the treasury. One was Rome's first aqueduct—the aqua Appia—which brought fresh water to the city's people from the Sabine Hills, the Claudian clan's ancestral home. The other was the via Appia, which left the city not far from the spot at which the aqueduct entered. It's to the road proper that we can now turn.

Before we do, though, let's note that Appius gave both of these projects his name, creating for himself what a later observer called an "immortal monument" and setting an equally timeless precedent. Whereas older byways that existed as well-worn, ad hoc paths were known for the direction in which they led (as the via Ardeatina led to the town of Ardea) or the commodities transported on them (so the via Salaria was the Salt Road), after Appius all roads built with public funds carried the name of the Roman magistrate who initiated them. But while those later statesmen gave the projects their clan names—the via Flaminia, for example, built by the censor Gaius Flaminius not quite a century after the via Appia was begun—Appius chose to use his first name. Perhaps *this* was a mark of Claudian pride: for while most first names, like Gaius or Marcus, were utterly undistinctive—they might in fact belong to any Tom, Dick, or Harry—in the late fourth century BCE the first name Appius belonged by tradition only to the Claudii.

ROAD OF POWER

Reg: They've bled us white, the bastards. They've taken every-
    thing we had, not just from us, from our fathers and from
    our fathers' fathers. . . . And what have they ever given us in
    return?
Xerxes: The aqueduct.
Reg: Oh yeah, yeah they gave us that. Yeah. That's true.
Masked Activist: And the sanitation!

Stan: Oh yes . . . sanitation, Reg—you remember what the city
    used to be like.
Reg: All right, I'll grant you that the aqueduct and the sanitation
    are two things that the Romans have done . . .
Matthias: And the roads . . .
Reg (sharply): Well yes, obviously the roads . . . the roads go
    without saying . . .

Monty Python's *Life of Brian*

Aqueducts, sewers, roads—obviously the roads, the roads go without
saying—the three most visible and distinctive footprints of Roman
civilization: two of the three were initiated by Appius Claudius Caecus as censor in 312. It was of course no accident that Appius began
his road in the midst of a period of Roman expansion. In another
two generations Rome would come to possess its first overseas province, Sicily, and after another century it would dominate the Mediterranean. The Appia was at once an instrument and a manifestation
of Rome's growing power.

Even by the time its kings were overthrown at the end of the sixth
century, Rome was a regional power, with direct influence over the
Alban Hills to the east and the Tiber Valley down to the sea. The
city also enjoyed alliances with the other peoples of Latium (the La-
tini, who like the Romans spoke Latin), while its commercial and
diplomatic ties extended well beyond central Italy. And by the next
century Rome was using conquest and colonization to bring the rest
of Latium under its control. Its expansion continued throughout the
fourth century and the first quarter of the third, in what are called
the Italian Wars.

The main episodes can be sketched quickly. First, a three-year
war with the Latins and their allies from farther south (341–338) re-
sulted in a catastrophe for the Latins. Some of their towns were ab-
sorbed directly into the Roman political fabric, with full citizenship,
while others were left as nominally independent allies who enjoyed
rights of trade and intermarriage with the Romans. Even before that

war, however, the Romans had started to come into conflict with the Samnites, a federation of bellicose tribal clusters that had migrated under pressure from farther north and moved into the rugged territory of central Italy to the east and south of Latium. Starting in the 340s and continuing on and off for fifty years, the Romans fought a series of wars against the Samnites and their allies, until their victory in 295 against a combined force of Samnites, Gauls, Etruscans, and others left Rome the dominant power on the whole of the Italian peninsula save the ancient Greek settlements of the far south. Three centuries later, when a statue of Appius Claudius joined other Roman culture heroes in the Forum of Augustus, the accompanying inscription, written by the emperor himself, recalled his feats as consul in the last stages of these wars:

> Appius Claudius
> Caecus, the son of Gaius,
> censor, twice consul . . .
> took many towns from the Samnites
> [and] put the Sabines' and Etruscans' army to rout.

The end of the Samnite Wars, and control over the Samnites themselves, gave Rome the security and the manpower to compete with Carthage and, ultimately, to control the Mediterranean. In history's zero-sum game, the Samnites' defeat was absolutely pivotal in the story of what Rome was to become.

The Greek settlements of the south fell next. In 281 Tarentum (now Taranto), a city of great wealth and high culture, called upon King Pyrrhus of Epirus, on the Greek mainland, to protect his Hellenic kinsmen in Magna Graecia. Pyrrhus, probably expecting to pick off some low-hanging Italian fruit, invaded with a force of twenty-five thousand infantry, three thousand cavalry, and twenty elephants, and in fact his invasion brought some initial setbacks to the Romans. Yet Appius Claudius, now aged and blind (*caecus*, hence his final name), spoke strongly and successfully against making a peace of convenience, and those initial successes cost the victor himself dearly, giving posterity the phrase "Pyrrhic victory." In 275 Rome shocked the Greek world by defeating Pyrrhus's army at Maloentum, a Samnite stronghold in central Italy. The town was soon made a Roman colony, and its name, which sounded to the Roman ear like Maleventum, "Bad Outcome," was changed to Beneventum, "Good Outcome." A few years later, in 272, Tarentum itself was captured. The time that had elapsed between the first conflicts with the Samnites and the capitulation of Tarentum was no more than a single lifetime—to be precise, the lifetime of Appius Claudius Caecus.

So you can imagine why in this period a well-built road running south from Rome, first to the very threshold of the Samnites' territory and ultimately through Tarentum, would have been a timely thing. In fact, the year in which Appius Claudius began the road, 312, fell squarely in the middle of the Second Samnite War (326–304), and we can see how the stages in which it was built follow the course of Rome's expansion southward.

The first segment, from Rome to Capua (modern Santa Maria Capua Vetere) in northern Campania, spanned 121 miles, linking the city to its Campanian allies at a point only a day's march from their current enemies.* The route moved in an almost perfectly straight line from Rome southeast to Tarracina (now Terracina), a colony on the coast. After arcing inland across the Plain of Fundi (Fondi) and through the Monti Aurunci, it rejoined the coast and ran farther south to Sinuessa (Mondragone), then turned inland for good and made for Capua.

Like neighboring Minturnae (Minturno) back up the road toward Rome, Sinuessa became a Roman colony in 296, and the two were strategically important garrisons of citizen-soldiers poised against the Samnite threat. When that threat had been removed, the road was

---

*Capua itself, a rich city and an untrustworthy ally, had shown signs of disaffection after a Roman setback in 315; a century later, during the Second Punic War, Capua would defect to Hannibal and become a threat, but that is another story.

extended another thirty miles to Beneventum (now Benevento), after it too became a colony in 268. From there it ultimately stretched down the spine of the peninsula, through Venusia (Venosa) (a colony since 291) to grand Tarentum, a distance of about 163 miles, then turned east and north to run the remaining 40 miles across Italy's heel to Brundisium, the port that became another colony in 240 and gave Rome an opening onto the Adriatic Sea and the Greek mainland beyond.

When completed, the Appia covered roughly 353 miles, a journey of about two weeks for a lightly burdened traveler making good time.* A glance at any relief map of Italy will show that most of those miles must have carried a high price tag in sweat and ingenuity. We say that the Apennines run "down the middle" of the peninsula, but really, that is misleading. Below the broad expanse of the Po Valley and the Veneto in the north, the map shows only occasional pockets of green among the brown and white ruffles and ridges that dominate. A small fraction of the Appia—the stretch in southern Latium down to Tarracina, another stretch along the coast, the approaches to Tarentum and Brundisium—ran along the map's green bits, and not a small portion of those green bits were marshland. Building the road did not just assert the permanence of Roman military and political power in Italy, it asserted Rome's ability to dominate, even change, the landscape of Italy itself. No wonder that in considering such an achievement the elder Pliny compared the Romans' roads with the pharaohs' pyramids, and not to the pyramids' advantage ("a useless and stupid display of wealth").

The engineering challenges were enormous, and the planning alone must have required months. To take just the thirty-seven miles that run from the Alban Hills in Latium down to Tarracina, the stretch of road there was so straight, the surveying so precise, that Italians call the modern road that follows its course the "Fettucina,"

---

*According to the historian Procopius, writing in the sixth century CE, such a traveler would spend five days on the leg between Rome and Capua.

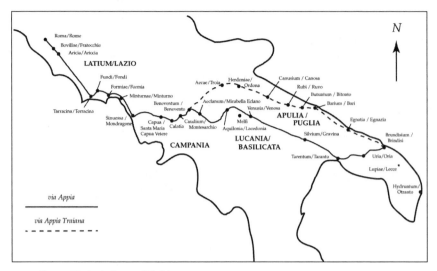

N

Figure 3. Via Appia, Rome to Brindisi

after the very straight and medium-broad pasta it evokes—and much of that razor-sharp precision was achieved over the Pomptine Marshes, terrain that first had to be channeled and stabilized to give the road a firm foundation. That the 121 miles to Capua were completed in only five years, as seems to have been the case, suggests that once the planning had been completed, the actual construction was contracted out to the locals, so that work on the several segments could go forward simultaneously—an arrangement that would have extended Appius Claudius's role as patron, and with it the pool of his clients and supporters, far south beyond the city.

Not only did marshes need to be channeled, but embankments, too, had to be built to elevate the roadway in places liable to suffer periodic flooding. At least half a dozen significant rivers crossed the route and needed bridging, and there were any number of smaller streams that had to be diverted. Cuttings had to be made to bring the road through the hills and mountains. And then there was the roadbed itself and, ultimately, the paving. Just listing the challenges prompts the urge to go lie down, and there are certainly too many

Figure 4. The "Fettucina"

such challenges—a book's worth by themselves—to talk about here. But to allow us to imagine the road "all the way down" before we start to walk on it, we should spend a few moments at least on the roadbed and the paving.

To create the roadbed, the margins were marked out and three trenches were dug, two narrow drainage ditches on either side of the margins and the broad central trench for the road itself. This trench was eleven yards wide or more (dimensions found in the most ancient parts of the road that have been excavated), and deep enough— usually a yard to a yard and half—to reach a stable base, which was made as level as possible and tamped down by hand. This base was then covered with sand or with a three-inch layer of lime mortar— a compound of lime, cement, sand, and water, also used for building—which was smoothed by hand and allowed to harden.

Three different kinds of stone were then laid on this foundation: first, fairly large stones at least two inches thick set with more lime

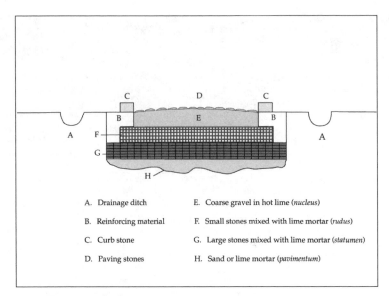

A. Drainage ditch

B. Reinforcing material

C. Curb stone

D. Paving stones

E. Coarse gravel in hot lime (*nucleus*)

F. Small stones mixed with lime mortar (*rudus*)

G. Large stones mixed with lime mortar (*statumen*)

H. Sand or lime mortar (*pavimentum*)

Figure 5. Cross-section of road

mortar in two layers; then, a layer of smaller stones or gravel mixed with lime mortar or sand that was leveled and tamped down; and finally, coarse gravel mixed with hot lime laid on in several layers that were compacted and crowned, to ensure that water would run off. If there was paving (we'll get to that soon), it was laid in this last layer of gravel.

Since each of the three layers of stone was narrower than the base on which it was laid, each side of the road was bordered by a terraced embankment, which was filled with blocks or rubble for reinforcement. Curbstones were set to mark off a pedestrian walkway on both sides. The segments of the ancient roadway that are visible today are regularly just over thirteen feet wide, consistent with the testimony of Procopius that two wagons going in opposite directions could pass each other—and in fact on a portion of the road near Rome I have seen, not two wagons, but a Fiat and a horse-drawn sulky do just that.

Now, a simple back-of-the-envelope calculation shows that if the main trench for the roadbed was dug (say) a yard deep and eleven yards wide on average, every mile of road laid required that not quite 523,000 cubic feet of earth be moved: multiply that by the 121 miles between Rome and Capua, and the total comes to about 63,250,000 cubic feet, all dug by hand. (To anticipate your question: the volume of the Great Pyramid at Giza is roughly 91,600,000 cubic feet.) But those numbers are misleading in several respects. The method of construction was not absolutely uniform but differed from place to place and time to time: often there might be two, not three, layers of stone over the roadbed's base; here and there the road might be narrower; in rural areas there might not be walkways; and so on. So in that respect the numbers might be taken to overstate the case. But mostly, and more dramatically, they are misleading in the opposite direction. For one thing, those numbers represent only the material that was taken *away*: to account for the material that was brought in to make the road, those figures must be nearly doubled. For another thing, the distance between Rome and Capua represents only a third of the Appia's total length: so now triple the numbers you just doubled. (The Great Pyramid begins to seem a dwarf.) And then there are the mountains. And the paving.

In the next chapter we will take a walk on the mile and a half or so of the Appia that has been excavated in the Monti Aurunci between Fondi (ancient Fundi) and Formia (Formiae). It is a very beautiful and enlivening walk, our favorite on the southern leg of the trip, for reasons I hope to convey. Here, though, I am thinking only of brute force. The road climbs, mountains hover on both sides, and you see the green growth at their lower levels giving way to gray-brown rock above. As Fondi slips away behind you, the hillside that the roadway is traversing rises steeply off to your right and drops off to your left. But of course you yourself are not tipping off to the left or leaning into the hill on your right to keep your balance as you walk. You are walking uphill on perfectly level ground, thanks to the massive job of terracing that the Romans did when they first cut the roadway through these mountains. To a height of twenty feet and more on the mountain side, and to a breadth of thirty feet and more, all the earth and stone were simply cut away—though "simply" hardly does justice to such work in a world without explosives, where having to rely on human muscle wielding iron picks and wedges made the going torturously slow. The muscle belonged to slaves and criminals, who were not expected to survive the experience: it was not for nothing that being condemned to build and maintain the roads was considered a punishment that ranked with being condemned to work the mines or to face the beasts in the arena.

So another back-of-the-envelope calculation: first, imagine a triangular figure with a height of at least twenty feet, a base of at least thirty feet, and a depth of one foot; then project that figure out over the 5,280 feet that make up a mile. For every mile of roadway laid in these hills, at least 1,600,000 cubic feet of earth and stone had to be removed before the roadbed itself could be dug. Not that the material was wasted, at least on this stretch of the road. It was used as backfill between the terrace and the walls—the enormous walls, in places fifty feet high and running on for hundreds of yards—that were raised to reinforce the roadway and protect it from erosion: massive blocks of stone joined by concrete, dating to the time of Appius Claudius, still there today. All this for a modest stretch of road in not very special hill country; and so much of the road passed through hill country just like this.

And when they had cut through the hillside, raised the walls, dug the trench, laid in the layers of stone and gravel, then they could haul in the blocks for paving on mule-drawn carts. Except that they did not, at least not at first. When the road from Rome to Capua was first completed, its surface was compacted gravel, and it stayed that way over most of the road's course for at least a generation. A symbolically important segment was paved with stone blocks in 295, the first mile that led from the porta Capena in the city wall to the temple of Mars—the city's god of war and the father of Romulus—outside the city walls. Three years later the next twelve miles, to the suburban village of Bovillae (now Fratocchie), were paved with basalt. When the job of paving was completed is not clear; it probably was done in stages, with different stone (limestone is also known to have been used) along different segments of the road. Moving great masses of stone very long distances by land would have been very time-consuming and expensive, so on most parts of the route local materials were preferred where they were available. And as Mounts Vesuvius and Aetna remind us, this part of the Mediterranean was once the center of intense volcanic activity, providing vast deposits of basalt in central Italy. This became the stone of choice, and every piece of the original road I've been able to walk—in Rome, Terracina, the Monti Aurunci, Minturno—has the same dark gray look and smooth feel. The stone was quarried in pyramidal chunks, each chunk with a rounded base a foot or more across and an apex of perhaps half that. Set in the gravel with apex down, base up, and fitted together—though Procopius said that they did not look so much fitted together as grown together—they provided a surface very different from the irregular, even jagged, feel of the stone roads built by the Inca, who did not know the wheel. The Appia, by contrast, was all about wheels: among the first sights that strike a traveler on the Appia today are the grooves worn by the countless wagons that ground along the same path, century after century after century.

It's the right time, I think, to take that path.

ROAD OF PEACE

The bus swung round and came to a stop. For this leg of our exploring we had decided not to repeat yesterday's ugly and terrifying walk over the Appia's first three Roman miles. Instead, a ride on the Metro and then the bus deposited us at the Cecilia Metella stop at 8:30 on a Sunday morning in late April. If we turned right, toward the northwest, a couple of hundred yards would bring us to the grand tomb of the lady for whom the stop is named (we'll get there, but not just yet). Instead, we turned left and headed southeast, away from the city and out toward the Roman countryside.

Figure 6. Stone pines

Though the sun was high enough to warm the air, the first few hundred yards were still mostly in shadow, thanks to the high walls that continued to crowd the Appia on each side and the broad canopies of the old stone pines. I love these trees, Mediterranean natives that produce spherical cones the size of softballs and look nothing like most North American pines. Years ago, when I first read the younger Pliny's account of Vesuvius's eruption and saw him compare the rising cloud of smoke and ash to a pine tree, I was puzzled because I hadn't yet seen one of these: he was describing what we'd call a mushroom cloud.

Soon, the high walls yielded to open fence-work or the low stone walls that date to the mid-nineteenth century, and we were bathed in golden springtime light. The air was fresh, the sun and breeze were warm on our faces, a profusion of wildflowers waved in the wind—yellow and lavender flowers I couldn't name, and thousands of brilliant poppies—and there was perfect quiet, broken only by the birdsong and our occasional murmured conversation. We walked on in complete peace, happy to share the road with the occasional jogger or cyclist, happy even to share it with the occasional plane gliding in low to land at Ciampino Airport beyond the modern road, the via Appia Nuova, a couple of miles off to the left.

The feeling of peace becomes more intense in those spots where the ancient roadway descends to a level a couple of yards below the grade of the surrounding terrain. In these passages—especially if you're short, as I am—walking below grade brings a greater focus to the experience, as the world around is for a time sealed off by the rising ground on both sides. Apart from a couple of gentle curves, the course of the road is very straight, and an ancient lava flow guarantees that it remains very level, with a dip and then a rise before the seventh milestone.

As the morning passed, the traffic of cyclists and joggers became thicker, the cyclists mostly sticking to paths worn in the earth on either side of the road. (Strike one of the basalt paving stones with your front wheel while your bottom is planted on the seat: really, not a pretty thought.) There was even the occasional auto, from one of the estates that border the road, but they moved very carefully indeed, because careless drivers pay a steep price. Near one of the modern crossroads we came upon a spot where a low-slung car had left a chunk of its undercarriage lying on the basalt, and a thick trail of blue-black oil marked the hundred yards it had traveled before turning onto the crossroad: how far had the driver gone, I wondered, before making the discovery that ruined his day? But just after midday the call of Sunday dinner emptied the route again. Footfall after footfall, the rhythm enfolded us, soothed us, refreshed us. Alone, with the Roman countryside spread out on both sides, we could for a while try on the feeling of being ancient.

Now, the Appia has not always evoked in modern visitors the sense of peace and contentment that we enjoyed as we made our way. Here is Charles Dickens's take from 1844, registered on an excursion made over the same ground and beyond, as recounted in his *Pictures from Italy:*

Figure 7. Via Appia, mile 4

One day, we walked out, a little party of three, to Albano, fourteen miles distant; possessed by a great desire to go there, by the
ancient Appian way, long since ruined and overgrown. We started
at half past seven in the morning, and within an hour or so, were
out upon the open Campagna. For twelve miles, we went climbing
on over an unbroken succession of mounds, and heaps, and hills,
of ruin. Tombs and temples overthrown and prostrate; small fragments of columns, friezes, pediments; great blocks of granite and
marble; mouldering arches, grass-grown and decayed; ruin enough
to build a spacious city from; lay strewn about us. . . . Now, we
tracked a piece of the old road, above the ground; now traced it,
underneath a grassy covering, as if that were its grave; but all the
way was ruin. In the distance, ruined aqueducts went stalking on

their course along the plain; and every breath of wind that swept towards us, stirred early flowers and grasses, springing up, spontaneously, on miles of ruin. The unseen larks above us, who alone disturbed the awful silence, had their nests in ruin; and the fierce herdsmen, clad in sheepskins, who now and then scowled out upon us from their sleeping nooks, were housed in ruin. The aspect of the desolate Campagna in one direction where it was most level, reminded me of an American prairie; but what is the solitude of a region where men have never dwelt, to that of a Desert, where a mighty race have left their footprints in the earth from which they have vanished. . . . Returning, by the road, at sunset, and looking, from the distance, on the course we had taken in the morning, I almost felt . . . as if the sun would never rise again, but looked its last, that night, upon a ruined world.

The high Romantic melancholy—"ruin . . . ruin . . . ruin . . . ruin . . . ruin"—is a bit over the top for my taste, the footprints of the mighty, vanished race too evocative of Shelley's "Ozymandias":

"Look on my works, ye Mighty, and despair!"
Nothing besides remains.

I find Henry James's take, in his *Italian Hours*, more congenial:

More and more beautiful as you get well away from the walls and the great view opens out before you—the rolling green-brown dells and flats of the Campagna, the long, disjointed arcade of the aqueducts, the deep-shadowed blue of the Alban Hills, touched into pale lights by their scattered towns.

That said, I see Dickens's point.

In fact the atmosphere that envelopes the Appia near Rome today, and gives it the feeling of a park, is a recent phenomenon and not at all ancient. Engravings and photographs from the nineteenth and early twentieth centuries show a landscape considerably more barren than the one a traveler now finds, with many fewer trees and shrubs and, it seems, more rubble strewn about. When Dickens made his excursion the route had scarcely begun to recover from the neglect into which it had fallen. By the time Rome's administration crumbled in the fifth century CE, the land surrounding the Appia near Rome had come to be held by the church, as it would later be held by a succession of great families. A long period of decline followed: maintenance ceased, traffic decreased, and by the fourteenth century the route was more or less abandoned. It was only from the mid-eighteenth century that antiquarians and historians began to take a disciplined interest in the Appia's past. Francesco Maria Pratilli published the first description of the road's full course, from Rome to Brindisi, in 1745. Four decades later, in November 1786, Goethe recorded in his diary impressions of the monuments he saw on his Italian journeys of 1786–1788:

> Today I visited . . . the Circus of Caracalla, the ruined tombs along the Via Appia and the tomb of Metella, which made me realize for the first time what solid masonry means. These people built for eternity; they omitted nothing from their calculations except the insane fury of the destroyers for whom nothing was sacred.

The Venetian sculptor Antonio Canova established an important precedent during explorations he undertook in 1808, winning from the papal authorities permission to allow the remains of monuments he uncovered to stay on site. (Most of the original inscriptions and sculptures have long since been removed to museums and replaced with replicas, to frustrate thieves.) But it was only in 1850, six years after Dickens's visit, that serious work began to reclaim the road, with Pope Pius IX putting his patronage behind the effort.

The key figure here was Luigi Canina, an architect and archaeologist from northern Italy who had conducted important excavations in Tusculum, the hill town east of Rome where Cicero and other prominent Romans kept their villas as refuges from the capital's heat. Canina worked fast: within three years he had completed extensive excavations between the fourth and ninth milestones and published, in two elegant volumes, an illustrated survey of the first part of the Appia out to Bovillae, beyond the twelfth milestone. In the process he reclaimed significant segments of the ancient road, brought some new objects to light and restored others, managed to appropriate ten yards of land on each side of the roadway proper, and set in place the low stone walls that run for long stretches from about the fourth milestone out, giving the road the feel of a specially designated zone that anticipated the modern park.

Canina's work was responsible for much of the look of the road as it is today, creating the posed appearance that some of the monuments have and assembling a series of architectural montages in which bits and pieces of ancient stone are set in broad façades of brick. Other sites have more recently been extensively reclaimed. Before the emperor Maxentius drowned near the Milvian Bridge in 312, when his defeat by Constantine the Great opened the way for the Christianization of the Empire, he had built a massive racing arena just before the third milestone, the Circus of Maxentius.* He had also begun next to it an almost equally massive palace that is being excavated today. After his defeat, the practically-minded craftsmen working on the palace crossed the Appia and went to work on a project of Constantine's on the other side.

A little farther along, some baths built by the wealthy Athenian sophist Herodes Atticus, in the second century, are also being excavated. Then there is the famous villa of the Quintilii, out by the fifth milestone, on a parcel of land acquired by the state in 1985. The Quintilii were two fabulously wealthy brothers who came from what

---

*Goethe and his contemporaries thought it belonged to another emperor, Caracalla.

Figure 8. Via Appia, mile 5

is now western Turkey and established themselves at Rome as patrons of culture and as political forces to be reckoned with, holding
the consulship together in 151 CE and later governing the provinces
of Greece and Asia. The suburban villa they built together was the
largest found along the Appia, situated on the same volcanic plateau
as the road and enjoying panoramic views to the east and south. Its

sprawling yet exquisite residential and bath complexes so aroused the emperor Commodus's envy that in 183 he trumped up charges against the brothers, had them executed, and confiscated the estate.

Most of all, though, there are the tombs.

ROAD OF DEATH

Between the porta San Sebastiano and the ninth milestone there are substantial remains of at least ninety-nine monuments, of which seventy-five have been identified as sepulchers, mausolea, and other repositories of the dead—only the tiniest fraction of the funerary monuments that literally lined the road in antiquity. Because the monuments were so densely crowded, the thing that a visitor will probably like most about walking the Appia today—the experience of the open Roman *campagna* on both sides of the road—is actually most false to the ancient road, while the segments closest to the city, where walls loom on either side, more truly capture the feeling of the past. For mile after mile beyond the city's gates—in fact as far as Casal Rotondo, an immense circular tomb just before the sixth milestone—the Appia was hemmed in by a nearly unbroken wall of tombs.

This is the aspect of the road that most captured the imagination of Nathaniel Hawthorne during an extended visit to Rome in the late 1850s, a few years after Luigi Canina's work. Here are some of the impressions recorded in his *French and Italian Notebooks*:

> The great ragged bulks of the tombs along the Appian Way now hove in sight, one with a farmhouse on its summit [the so-called "tomb of Geta," between the first and second milestones], and all of them preposterously huge and massive. . . . The tomb of Cecilia Metella came in sight a long while before we reached it, with the warm buff hue of its travertine. . . . After passing it, we saw an interminable line of tombs on both sides of the way, each of which might, for aught I know, have been as massive as that of Cecilia

Metella, and some perhaps still more monstrously gigantic, though now dilapidated and much reduced in size. . . . [W]e could go but a little father along this most interesting road, the borders of which are strewn with broken marbles, fragments of capitals, and nameless rubbish that once was beautiful. Methinks the Appian Way should be the only entrance to Rome—through an avenue of tombs.

Not that the Appia is unique in this respect. It just happens to make visible today a scene that would have met the traveler coming to Rome along any of its many roads.

How different this is from the space we make, without a second thought, for death and the dead in our own cities. If you walk the Freedom Trail in Boston, your tour will take you through Copp's Hill Burying Ground near the Old North Church, the Granary Burying Ground near the State House, and the King's Chapel and Burying Ground, all of them providing Bostonians with a final resting place in the heart of their city since long before the lamp was hung in the North Church tower to send Paul Revere on his ride. For that matter, a five-minute walk from my campus office will bring me to Princeton Cemetery, where I can contemplate the graves of Aaron Burr and all but a handful of Princeton University's deceased presidents, Burr's father among them (Woodrow Wilson is one of the absentees). I can assure you that the good men of classical Rome would be appalled.

A sacred boundary line surrounded Rome: the *pomerium*, originally marked out with a plow (according to legend) by Romulus himself and maintained, with occasional modifications, ever after, distinct from though partly coinciding with the line traced by the city walls. The line's significance was primarily religious, but as in most areas of Roman life, the religious and the political were intertwined in countless ways. The tribunes who served as protectors and patrons of Rome's commoners, the plebs, had their authority only within the *pomerium*, while for a commanding general to cross the *pomerium* and reenter the city was the equivalent of resigning his command.

Embracing and protecting Rome's civil community, the line distinguished the foreign from the domestic, the realm of war and violence from the realm of peace and law. (It was forbidden to carry a sword within the *pomerium:* so far as I'm aware, no Roman ever argued that if you outlaw swords, only criminals will have swords.) It also distinguished the world of the living from the place of the dead.

Ordinarily, no person could be buried inside the *pomerium,* above all because the dead were so problematic, in so many ways. They were, first of all, a source of pollution, not in a physical or environmental sense, but in a religious sense. A dead body was "matter out of place," as one famous definition of pollution puts it, and unfit to occupy the same space as the living and the gods above: corpses belonged to the gods below. Even handling the dead made a person ritually unclean and a source of pollution in his own right. In Roman towns the men who prepared dead bodies for their final disposition were themselves barred from living in town, and their civic status suffered from various official disabilities, like being disqualified from serving on the town council or holding public office.

The dead were also just very frightening. In classical Rome—the two centuries before and the two centuries after the turn of the common era, say—a dead person was not generally thought to have an afterlife as such a thing is imagined in some religions today, an unending existence in which the deceased retain their earthly identity and experience bliss or torment according to their earthly deserts. On the other hand, the dead did not have the decency to simply cease to exist. They belonged, as I said, to the gods below, and even, in one sense, *became* the gods below. The deceased lost their identity as individuals and were merged with the undifferentiated mass of all those who had ever died, the *di manēs,* the "good gods." If that curious, even empty-seeming epithet (who, after all, were the "*bad* gods"?) makes you suspect that the term might be a euphemism, that is because it is. Just as the Greeks called their Furies, the spirits of retribution that dwelt beneath the earth, the Eumenidēs—"kindly ones"—in the hope that euphemism would allow them to escape the dreaded ones' notice and avoid their awful powers, so the Romans referred to the "good gods" out of fear that they were anything but.

So the dead had to be kept away from the center of life, and there were several ways of seeing to this need. The most visible way produced the tombs that lined the road. Though the Romans had over the centuries disposed of their dead by both cremation and burial, by the first century BCE cremation had become the norm, and so it remained for three to four more centuries, during which there was a clear cultural divide in the Mediterranean basin. If you spoke Latin and lived in the western half, you burned your dead relations; if you spoke Greek and lived in the eastern half, you did not.

Cremation produces ash and bone, and disposing of the ash and bone while yet preserving them gave rise to the *columbarium*, or "dovecote," the modern term for the chamber-tomb that held a system of niches where the remains could be stored. Here's Hawthorne, again, on his visit to one of these chambers:

> A little farther towards the city we . . . came to the site of some ancient Columbaria, close by what seemed . . . a villa and a farmhouse. A man came out of the house and unlocked a door in a low building, apparently quite modern; but on entering we found ourselves looking into a large, square chamber, sunk entirely beneath the surface of the ground. A very narrow and steep staircase of stone, and evidently ancient, descended into the chamber; and, going down, we found the walls hollowed on all sides into little semicircular niches, of which, I believe, there were nine rows, one above another, and nine niches in each row. Thus they looked somewhat like the little entrance to a pigeon-house. . . . In every one of the . . . niches were two round holes covered with an earthen plate, and in each hole were ashes and little fragments of bones— the ashes and bones of the dead, whose names were inscribed in Roman capitals on marble slabs inlaid into the wall over each individual niche. . . . [T]he impression left on me was, that this mode of disposing of the dead was infinitely preferable to any which has

been adopted since that day. . . . I would rather have my ashes scattered over the soil to help the growth of the grass and daisies; but still I should not murmur much at having them decently pigeon-holed in a Roman tomb. . . . In [this tomb], measuring about twenty feet square, I roughly estimate that there have been deposited together the remains of at least seven or eight hundred persons, reckoning two little heaps of bones and ashes in each pigeon-hole, nine pigeon-holes in each row, and nine rows on each side.

The *columbarium* Hawthorne inspected held the remains of the freed slaves of Livia, wife of the emperor Augustus, and of other members of the imperial household, though it could as easily have been the collective tomb of a *collegium*, one of the organizations that poorer Romans joined to enjoy fellowship during life and to ensure that their remains would be treated decently after death. In any case, the practice of cremation faded over time, and by the third century the Romans had adopted the funeral practices of the Greek-speaking east, including the use of the sarcophagus, with its grim Greek name ("flesh-eater"). In the tomb's chamber, the small niches of the *columbarium* were replaced by larger niches into which these boxes of worked stone could be set. The change was not specifically inspired by the rise of Christianity, which was mostly critical of cremation as an obstacle to resurrection, but it was clearly congenial to it.

Though the change in custom dictated some changes in a tomb's internal organization, the resulting differences were negligible compared with the great variety of shapes and sizes that the tombs could take, and the different statements they could make. Besides the collective cremation tomb of the sort Hawthorne saw, with their chambers sunk underground, there were, much more commonly, individual or family tombs, and these might appear in any one of these forms: as an altar; as a small temple-like shrine (*aedicula*) set on a high base; as a cylindrical tower set atop one or more rectangular bases, wedding-cake fashion; as a two-story temple with a porch approached by a grand staircase; as a circular chamber with a cone-shaped roof; as a rectangular chamber with a cellar and two stories on top; or as a circular, brickwork mausoleum with a domed ceiling.

Some of these tombs were very grand indeed, but smaller monuments shouldered their way in to claim space among the giants. The point was to make the most striking public statement that your means allowed along the road of power, and thereby associate yourself and your kin with the grandeur that was Rome. "So-and-so made this *sibi suisque*," the inscriptions commonly say: "for himself and his own." The inscriptions also commonly address the passers-by, calling on them to stop, pay attention, show respect.

The most imposing and best preserved of the tombs belonged to the woman whose name has already been invoked several times, Caecilia Metella—or, to give her the full measure of dignity that the inscription on the tomb claims for her:

CAECILIAE

Q·CRETICI·F

METELLAE CRASSI

To Caecilia Metella, daughter of Quintus Creticus, wife of Crassus

Like any proper Roman woman, Caecilia Metella was known by the men who surrounded her, and these men had names that were among the grandest in Rome of the first century BCE. Her father's full and formal name was Quintus Caecilius Metellus Creticus. The first name, like Roman first names in general, had the same character as first names in European and North American culture today (women did not get a first name), while the second name, like our surnames, designated a person's family or clan. The third name, Metellus, began as a kind of nickname (it means something like "mercenary"), which the original owner's descendents then adopted to distinguish their branch of the Caecilian clan from others. The Caecilii Metelli first came to prominence early in the third century BCE, when Appius Claudius was approaching old age, and from that point on you could not swing a cat on the Roman political scene without hitting one: the "Index of Careers" in Robert Broughton's great *Magistrates of the Roman Republic*, the bible of this period for people like me, lists no fewer than thirty of them, including five censors and eighteen consuls, with Creticus himself winning a place among the consuls in 69.

As for the fourth name, "Creticus"—now *that* was special. The effect of it is comparable to "Lawrence of Arabia" or, perhaps better, "Gordon of Khartoum." It meant that this Quintus Metellus had conquered Crete and organized it as a Roman province, in the mid-60s. The custom of using a geographical epithet to burnish the name of a man who had gained military glory in a given region is illustrated most famously by Publius Cornelius Scipio Africanus, "Scipio of Africa," whose defeat of Hannibal at the battle of Zama in North Africa (202 BCE) ended the Second Punic War. It was a custom that bestowed more glory on the Caecilii Metelli than on any other clan: besides Creticus, the latest in this line, we also have (in chronological order) a Macedonicus, a Balearicus, a Delmaticus, and a Numidicus. The family's triumphal names allow us to trace Rome's expansion into every corner of the Mediterranean, from the Balearic Islands in the west, through Numidia in Africa, to Macedon, Dalmatia, and Crete in the east.

A woman from such a family did not marry just anyone. She was the nearest thing to a princess that a republic could produce, her dowry would bring a fortune, and deciding where to settle the princess and her dowry had dynastic implications, a chance to forge or strengthen ties to another family with plenty of dignity and clout. A shrewd father, Creticus decided to place his daughter with the family in Rome that least needed the dowry.

Her husband was one of the Licinii Crassi, a family of somewhat less political luster than the Caecilii Metelli, with only half as many listings in Broughton's "Index" and no offices recorded before the late third century. (The first Licinius to be called Crassus was evidently chubby, for that is what *crassus* means: like so many of the nicknames that the Romans liked to hang on each other—and keep!—it picks out an unflattering physical trait.) But whatever its relative handicap when it came to ancient consulships, this branch of the Licinii had one big thing going for it at the time of Caecilia Metella's marriage: her husband was almost certainly Marcus Licinius Crassus, the elder son of a father with the same name who was one of the great white sharks of Roman political life in the middle of the first century. A contemporary of Creticus, the elder Crassus had put down the slave revolt led by Spartacus that had terrified Italy in the years 73–71, then served as consul in 70 and censor in 65. He was also the prime mover in forming the alliance with the two other great white sharks of the day—Pompey the Great and Julius Caesar—that informally but effectively controlled Roman politics through much of the 50s. And he was rich beyond the dreams of greed, even at a time when the staggering influx of wealth from Rome's Empire encouraged the greedy to dream very big. His interests, overt and sub rosa, extended everywhere, and the ruthlessness with which he pursued them predictably inspired some invidious stories. One story, very possibly true, held that he formed a private fire-fighting company (Rome had no such public force at the time), which would appear at the scene of a fire, then dicker over the fee with the desperate owner while his building burned. Another story, very likely false, reported that after he was killed by the Parthians, Rome's imperial rival to the east, while leading a glory-hungry military campaign in 54–53, the enemy poured molten gold down his dead throat, in mockery of his greed.

We do not know when Caecilia Metella married young Crassus. For that matter, we do not know when she was born or died, or even whether it was her first marriage. But if we assume that it was, we can make some rough yet educated guesses. The young man served with Julius Caesar in 54, during Caesar's conquest of Gaul, and the office he held required him to have been at least thirty years old. So let's suppose that he was in fact born in 84 (a man with his connections would not be kept waiting for preferment), and let's recall that young women among the Roman elite typically married in their midteens, to a man five to ten years their senior. If we conclude that Caecilia Metella was born in the early 70s and married in the late 60s, it would square with the one other thing we know about her: she became the mother of yet another Marcus Licinius Crassus, who became consul in the year 30—and not just any consul, but the colleague of Julius Caesar's adoptive son, Gaius Julius Caesar Octavianus, known today as Octavian. Just the year before, Octavian had become the last strongman left standing after two decades of civil war, defeating Antony and Cleopatra in a naval battle at Actium, off the western coast of Greece. Three years later a grateful senate gave him the name Augustus, and over the next four decades he changed the world as no one since Alexander the Great had done three hundred years before, and as very, very few statesmen or soldiers have done since.

So as the world changed around them, the Licinii Crassi continued to do very well indeed, and Caecilia Metella evidently shared in their prosperity. Granted, not all was happiness amid the wealth and power. She apparently lost her husband while still in her thirties: we last hear of him in 48, and since he did not gain the consulship that would certainly have been his had he lived, we have to assume that he was dead before the end of the decade. If that's so, it's clear that she fulfilled the Roman ideal (more honored in the breach, perhaps, than in the observance) of remaining *univira*, a one-man woman: for she was still known as "the wife of Crassus" sometime in the century's final decades when her bones and ashes were shut away in her tomb.

And what a tomb it is. Built on a circular plan, it has a drum nearly a hundred feet in diameter and over thirty-five feet high, set upon a tall, square stone base that makes it still more imposing. The ensemble, in antiquity, would have been topped off by a conical dome. It is not Napoleon's tomb, to be sure, nor even Grant's, in its sheer dimensions, but since it sits near the crest of the rise as the Appia climbs toward the third milestone and a view of the volcanic plateau beyond, it dominated the horizon of travelers coming from Rome, set off in its visual field by the drum's cladding of trav-

Figure 9. Tomb of Caecilia Metella

ertine, still miraculously intact. As Hawthorne put it, "The tomb of Cecilia Metella came in sight a long while before we reached it." By the time they came within ten paces, travelers would be able to see clearly the sculpted frieze running round the top of the drum— ox skulls (*bukrania*, symbolic of sacrifice) and festoons in alternation—and then, in fine Pentelic marble quarried near Athens, three plaques, two in the form of trophies (one of these now missing) and the third, in the center, bearing the inscription that proclaims the princess's name and standing.

Caecilia Metella's remains are many centuries gone, and the conical dome is long gone, too, for reasons that have less to do with the ravages of time and the elements than with the way that the past along the Appian Way keeps impinging upon the present, and being repurposed by it. As the tomb dominated the view of a traveler laboring uphill toward it, so the view from the tomb commanded the surrounding landscape in a way that begged to be fortified: that is why the dome is gone, replaced by a crenellated battlement. The tomb was probably already fortified not long after the fifth or sixth century, and by the eleventh century it had been incorporated by the counts of Tusculum in a defensive settlement that sat astride the Appia, its entrance and exit blocking the road, turning back any traveler who came that way.

Three centuries later the property came into the possession of the princely Caetani family with the help of Pope Boniface VIII (a Caetani by birth), and the walls of the castle they built, attached to the tomb fore and aft, are still intact. And so it went, the monument passing through the hands of another half dozen families—and narrowly escaping demolition, by papal order, in 1589—until it was taken over by the state. Today, the central, conical *cella* where Caecilia Metella's remains came to rest is open to the sky, its brickwork interior a literal *columbarium*, the roost of pigeons.

All the grand tombs had stories like this to tell, of distinction in life recorded in pride after death. But as I said before, there was a kind of democracy in death, too, that allowed more humble people to claim a place along the road. If Caecilia Metella stood at the tip-top of the social pyramid of those interred here, representatives of the pyramid's base are very much in evidence, too, among the slaves and, especially, the freedmen whose tombs sprang up in the empty spaces between the grandees' massive monuments.

Like ancient Greece, like America's antebellum South, Rome was a slave society, a society whose way of life could not be sustained, was in fact inconceivable to begin with, absent the support of the countless humans whom the Roman scholar Varro placed in the category of "speaking tool." Rome's wars of conquest, especially, brought slaves to Italy by the tens and then hundreds of thousands, but as in the case of the Americas, a vigorous slave trade also saw to their abundance, as one among any number of other commodities. From the second century BCE and continuing for the next six centuries (the rise of Christianity made no great difference) slaves were ubiquitous and indispensable, their use so ingrained in the culture that the commands a well-bred child should use in speaking to them are found in the primers that were the ancient equivalent of *Dick and Jane.* Among the upper classes, who owned slaves in large numbers, they worked the fields, cleaned the houses, prepared and served the meals, and emptied the chamberpots. They were secretaries and couriers, nurse-maids and tutors, body servants, whipping boys, and sexual toys. The way that slaves cushioned daily life and made it easy surely encour-aged, if it did not actually create, the petulant egoism and monstrous self-concern of the average Roman aristocrat, who would—I guar-antee—make the most arrogant and selfish of your acquaintances look like the Dalai Lama by comparison. Such a person could ex-pect his every desire to be satisfied, perfectly and right now, be-cause so many hands toiled, as good as unseen, to ensure that it was. Not that this much distinguishes Roman slavery from the slavery of Greece or the American South. But the Romans also did something distinctive—in fact, downright strange—with their slaves.

They freed them in huge numbers, a practice unheard of in the slave societies of Greece and the antebellum South. Some they freed at the time of their own death, as a magnanimous gesture in their wills. Others they freed because the slaves had saved one copper coin at a time, over years, to amass the price of their freedom. Still others they freed spontaneously, as a reward for meritorious service. They freed so many, in fact, that by the end of the first century BCE the emperor Augustus had a law enacted to limit the number that one man could liberate. But while the circumstances in which slaves were freed were many and varied, there were two constants.

First, there was the general rule that the chances of your gain-ing your freedom increased in direct proportion to your proximity to your master. If you worked as a field slave on a distant estate, your chances were essentially zero, unless your master freed his slaves en masse in his will. But if you were a house slave and survived to (say) thirty, the likelihood that you would be freed was enormous: the many freedmen whose tombs line the Appia would mostly have been slaves in their masters' residences in the capital.

The second constant lay with the consequence of being formally freed, which was always and everywhere the same. One moment you were a slave named Hermes or Eros, with no legal identity and no rights of your own; the next you were not merely your own man, you were a Roman citizen, now bearing the first two names of your former master—your new *patronus* (a term related to *pater*, "father")—and retaining your old slave-name as a nickname. Welcome to the *populus Romanus*, Marcus Tullius Hermes. There were a few limitations and conditions attached to your new freedom, to be sure: you promised to continue performing a certain amount of work for your *patronus*, for example, and you were not eligible to become a magistrate of the Roman people (though your sons were). But in most respects you had ceased to be a *puer*—a "boy," as slaves were commonly called—and were now a *vir*, an adult Roman man among men.

The sudden change in status must have been dizzying for the newly free citizens, but following the habits and customs of the masters they had served provided some stability. Property owning was one example. The "boy" who had had no legal existence as a person while enslaved, and so could own no property in his own name, now could buy and own whatever he could afford in the way of houses, clothing, and chattel: the former slave often became a slave owner in his turn. Education was another example: the poet Horace, a native of Venusia on the Appian Way, tells us how his father—a former slave who became prosperous as an auctioneer—chose not to have him schooled in his hometown, where he might be bullied by the burly sons of centurions, but sent him to Rome instead, to be (literally) whipped into shape by one of the most prominent teachers of the day and get the kind of training that distinguished the social and cultural elite.

This sort of assimilation also extended to the respectability of the tomb. While some freedmen chose to be interred with their former masters, many arranged for tombs of their own. One of my favorite examples along the Appia is found near the fifth milestone, on the right side of the road as you're heading away from town. There you will see the core of what used to be a substantial tower tomb, a tall pillar of conglomerate stone perhaps twenty-five feet high, set upon squared blocks of the volcanic tuff that's plentiful in the area. At the base of the tower is a well-cut inscription on a block of the same stone. The inscription is in the usual all-capitals style, with the raised dots ("interpuncts") used to separate words: the initial L in the first, third, and fifth lines stands for "Lucius," a very common Roman first name, and the abbreviation L·L at the end of the same lines stands for "L(ucii) l(ibertus)," "the freedman of Lucius." Three men, then, who were all once the slaves of a Lucius Valerius and took his name in the usual way, after they were freed. But it's the names on the second, fourth, and sixth lines that rivet the attention: Baricha, Zabda, and Achiba. Plainly Semitic and probably Jewish, the names all but invite you to imagine a story about their owners, or at least to ask some questions. Were the three men brothers or fellow townsmen before they were taken in slavery? How were they taken? Were they captured when Titus, son of the emperor Vespasian and future emperor himself, sacked Jerusalem in 70 CE, part of the loot that we see soldiers hauling off in the scenes carved on Titus's arch in the Forum? Or were they brought to Rome still earlier, on a slave dealer's ship? (Inscriptions like this one are very hard to date: first century CE seems to be the consensus, but nothing can be said beyond that.) Were they among a number of Lucius Valerius's freedmen buried in the same tomb? Or if so costly a tomb was theirs alone, how did they come to afford it? Had they been business partners in the years after slavery? In fact, might the Lucius Valerius Zabda recalled on this inscription be the same man as the Lucius Valerius Zabda mentioned on another first-century inscription from Rome—a former slave who became a slave dealer in his turn? But the mute stone, as spare and dignified in its own way as the marble plaque on Caecilia Metella's tomb, provides no answers to satisfy modern curiosity.

The scene along this avenue of tombs blended the grand, the grim, the holy, and the sordid, and summoning up how different elements looked in antiquity calls for different degrees of imagination. Pictur-

Figure 10. Freedmen's epitaph

ing the monuments themselves, gleaming stone and burnt sienna brick, is not very difficult once you have in mind the essential shapes that were used: altar, temple, tower, and the rest. It's also not hard to imagine the Rosalia, the festival of roses in May and June, when the bright flowers were placed on the tombs, or the Parentalia, the feast of ancestors, when each family made offerings to the spirits of their own dead. These nine days in February were "days of religious scruple" (*dies religiosi*), when weddings were forbidden, temples were closed, and magistrates did not wear their official dress: the ordinary practices of daily life were held in suspense as the people came out to the tombs to pay their respects. A passage from Ovid's poem on the calendar, the *Fasti*, helps us along here:

> Places of burial get their due respect, too: we appease our
> ancestors' souls
> and give little gifts to the tombs built for them.
> The Good Gods ask only a little: in place of a rich gift, piety pleases.
> The gods who dwell by the depths of the Styx are not greedy.

A small tile is enough, draped with an offering of garlands,
    some scattered kernels of wheat, a few grains of salt,
bread soaked in wine unmixed with water, a sprinkling of violets:
    leave the potsherd with these bits in the middle of the road.
Not that I rule out bigger gifts, but even these can appease the
    shades.

Of course there were witches here, too, but they are harder to summon up: fittingly, I suppose, because they did their work at night and went out of their way to avoid being seen. The remains of the dead— especially those who died violently or otherwise prematurely— had special powers ("Take the skull of a man who died a violent death," more than one ancient magic spell begins), and those who trafficked in such things skulked among the tombs. That was also one of the places where prostitutes worked their beat—and here almost no imagination at all is needed, because they still do. One afternoon, as we approached the modern crossroad near the ninth milestone, a young woman passed us heading back toward the city, her clothing a bit askew. And when we reached the crossroad there was a proper traffic jam, as a cluster of women led their clients this way and that into the bushes on either side of the road. "I don't understand," dear Laura said, "What are all these people doing? Is there a bathroom here?" Now it's true that—though she's seen plenty of the world's grimy side in her work, including time spent representing accused murderers—Laura has remained what the Romans would have called an *anima candida*, a pure soul. Here, though, it was not so much innocence at work as wishful thinking, since the park's lack of amenities happened to be much on her mind at the time.

With the rise of Christianity, the scene would have changed, more by addition than by subtraction. The Parentalia withered away over time, replaced by other rites of remembrance. The prostitutes surely remained. What was new were the churches in which the relics of the holy dead were buried and—mostly hidden from view underground—the catacombs, miles upon miles of them, where hundreds of thousands more were laid to rest.

The area along the Appia was made for these monuments. Jews accustomed to burying their dead in tombs cut from the rocks of their homeland continued that practice in the Diaspora, where they found the tuff around Rome—strong yet easy to work—well suited to the purpose. There were Jewish catacombs outside the city as early as the second century CE, and the Christians took these as their model. The first public Christian cemetery—from the Greek word *koimē-tērion*, "place of sleep"—was established by the deacon (later pope, then saint) Callixtus at the start of the third century, and it forms the oldest part of what are known as the catacombs of San Callisto today.

There are three modest Jewish catacombs in the vicinity of the via Appia near Rome: the archeological ministry maintains the most substantial of these, just off the road, within a modern vineyard. But even the largest of the Jewish catacombs, in the northeast quarter of the city on the grounds of the Villa Torlonia, is on a scale very different from that of the grand Christian cemeteries. Three dozen Christian catacombs are known, eight of them on or near the Appia, and while they vary in size, their design is essentially the same. You descend via steps to a barrel-vaulted gallery, where three or four tiers of tombs are cut, like the drawers of a lateral file, in the gallery wall: a pair of bodies was placed in each tomb, which was sealed with a slab of stone and (for the most part) left unmarked. Separate chambers for more prosperous families extend off the gallery at right angles, as do other galleries that lead to still other galleries, the whole network ramifying in an irregular, planless diffusion. When the galleries were extended as far as they could go, the people simply dug down and began a new network of galleries at a lower level.

The largest and most frequently visited catacombs on the Appia are those of San Sebastiano, between the second and third milestones, and San Callisto, closer to the city between San Sebastiano and the spot where the via Appia and the via Ardeatina meet. San Sebastiano gives us the term "catacomb" itself, first used in the fourth century to refer specifically to it as "the cemetery *ad catacumbas*" (perhaps "at the hollows": the word's origin is unknown, but it might refer to nearby clay quarries). The site takes its current name from Saint Sebastian, the martyr believed to be buried there, and it houses a splendid, larger-than-life-size *Bust of the Saviour* that has lately been identified as the last work of Gianlorenzo Bernini. Originally, though, the site was known as the "basilica of the apostles," because the remains of Saints Peter and Paul were thought to have been kept there for some decades. Because so many of the faithful wanted to be buried near the saints and draw on the grace channeled through their relics, seven and a half miles of galleries were ultimately dug. The catacombs of San Callisto also housed the bones of saints, including Saint Caecilia (no relation to the lady in the grand tomb) and, in the "chapel of the popes," the nine men who succeeded Callixtus in the course of the third century. Here there are ten miles of galleries dug on four different levels, from the early third century CE to the early fifth.

Even though the remains of the dead had long since been removed, visiting the catacombs in the time before electric lighting and good ventilation was clearly a trial. In his diary Goethe reported:

> My visit to the Catacombs . . . was not much of a success. I had hardly taken a step into that airless place before I began to feel uncomfortable, and I immediately returned to the light of day and the fresh air and waited . . . for the return of the other visitors.

Dickens, for his part, was again overwrought:

> A gaunt Franciscan friar, with a wild bright eye, was our only guide, down into this profound and dreadful place. The narrow ways and openings hither and thither, coupled with the dead and heavy air, soon blotted out, in all of us, any recollection of the track by which we had come; and I could not help thinking, "Good Heaven, if,

in a sudden fit of madness he should dash the torches out, or if he should be seized with a fit, what would become of us!" On we wandered, among martyrs' graves, passing great subterranean vaulted roads, diverging in all directions, and choked up with heaps of stones, that thieves and murderers may not take refuge there, and form a population under Rome, even worse than that which lives between it and the sun. Graves, graves, graves.

By contrast, the modern experience is brisk and efficient, so much so that it left me—for all that I'm a nonbeliever—chilled and a bit depressed. The operation at San Callisto is designed to process the maximum number of pilgrims in the minimum amount of time, and it works wonderfully well. Visitors are grouped according to language, and the group to which you are assigned waits until a critical mass has been reached and a guide who speaks your language is available: our English-language group included visitors from Scandinavia and was led by a young priest from Poland. He was personable and sincere, and did not in the least give the impression that he was now doing on autopilot what he had done hundreds of times before. But he plainly had a script, and that script included the directions "Keep them together" (thank goodness, of course: here I sympathize with Dickens) and "Keep them moving." We would pause at intervals, to receive an installment of the history of the place, and in this our guide was precise to an almost academic degree, for example scrupulously correcting the myth—repeated even by that arch-skeptic, Mark Twain, in *Innocents Abroad*—that Christians had actually lived in the catacombs during times of persecution.

We paused a bit longer in the crypt of the popes, regarded as the holiest place in the complex, and the faithful among us were plainly moved. But as I said, I ended a bit depressed: so much was said about the scale of the place, which is indeed astounding (perhaps a quarter million in capacity), that the individual humans who were once here became dwarfed and lost to view. As a lapsed Catholic and convert to Judaism, I do not share their belief, but I respect the intensity with which they kept to it, many of them to the point of death, because I know enough about the times to know how hard it often was for them to confess their Christian faith. The only contact I felt that I had with them, finally, came from occasional glimpses of the personal graffiti that other visitors had left more than a millennium ago: "O holy souls, remember Marcianus, Successus, Severus, and all our brothers . . ."

But the graffiti cheered me, too, because they reminded me that I was repeating, in a modern mode, the experience of countless other tourists, or pilgrims, that stretched back to antiquity. This was the layering of time and times, the meeting and interpenetration of past and present, that I was looking for on this trip: so just savor it, I said to myself. After all, the modern staircase that we had descended to reach the galleries followed the path of the staircase that Pope Damasus, a shrewd and polished promoter of the faith, had introduced in the second half of the fourth century, to make the martyrs' tombs more accessible to visitors. And he had converted the crypt of the popes into a chapel, complete with skylights and his own poems inscribed on the walls. Here is one of them:

> Seeker, know that here lies a legion of the blessed:
> reverend tombs contain the bodies of the saints,
> but their souls have been wafted aloft to heaven's royal palace.
> Here lies the company of Pope Sixtus [martyred in 258] with
>   trophies won from the enemy.
> Here the company of the elders [the popes] who guard the altars of
>   Christ. . . .
> Here young men and children, old men and their chaste
>   descendents
> who preferred to keep their virginal purity.
> Here too, I confess, I Damasus would wish to have been buried,
> did I not fear disturbing the holy ashes of the blessed.

And the seekers came for centuries, as we can see from the itineraries that have come down to us, the equivalent of ancient Fodor's guides. Here's an especially detailed tour of the holy sites the pilgrim could expect to find in the seventh century:

> Next to the Appian Way, in the eastern part of the city, is the church of the martyr St. Soter, where she herself lies with many martyrs. And next to the same Way is the church of St. Sixtus, the pope, where he himself sleeps. There too the virgin Caecilia rests, and there St. Tarsicius and St. Geferinus lie in a single tomb. And there St. Eusebius and St. Colocerus and St. Parthenius lie, each of them by himself. And 800 martyrs rest in the same place. Not far from there, in the cemetery of Callistus, Cornelius and Cyprian sleep in the church. . . . And next to the same Way is the church of St. Sebastian, where he himself sleeps [and] where there are tombs of the Apostles in which they rested for forty years; and there too the martyr Cyrinus is buried. In fact by the same road one reaches [Albano], which gives access to the church of St. Senator, where lie the bodily remains of both Perpetua and countless saints; and great miracles are accomplished in the same place.

This guide may date to the seventh century, but at its core is material that was already centuries old. The guidance that it gave would have continued to be useful until the ninth century. That is when most of the remains of the saints and martyrs were moved inside the city, and the Appia took another step, a big one, on the way to neglect and decline.

It was midafternoon now, and pretty damn warm for April. We had stopped in the shade on the side of the road, out beyond the sixth milestone, to read a funeral inscription, an old one dating to the first century BCE, that was among the many unearthed by Luigi Canina in his campaign of 1851. Resting upon a low façade of brick, the rectangular stone is cut about three times as wide as it is high, to accommodate the long lines of verse:

> Stop, stranger, and look at this little mound of earth on the left, where
> the bones of a good person are enclosed, one compassionate, devoted,
> of modest means. Please, traveler, do not mistreat this monument.
> Gaius Atilius Euhodus, a freedman of Serranus [and] a dealer in pearls
> from the Sacred Way, is buried in this monument. Traveler, farewell.
>
> According to my will no one may be placed and buried in this monument
> save those freedmen to whom I granted and assigned this in my will.

As jobs of self-presentation go, this one deserves solid marks for economy and effect. Formally, the tomb's occupant doesn't speak until the codicil of the last two lines: "I granted and assigned." Until that point we're to suppose that the monument itself speaks, or perhaps a disembodied voice of authority, to call on the traveler's attention, ask a kindness of him, and send him on his way. Formalities aside, I think we have the license to suppose that it's Euhodus's voice we hear throughout, saying the things he thinks it's most important for the passer-by to know.

Euhodus was once a slave of the Atilii Serrani, a political family of some prominence in the last two centuries BCE, standing a couple of steps below the preeminent Caecilii Metelli but far above the common run of men. After gaining his freedom, Euhodus had set himself up as a pearl dealer (*margaritarius*) in the center of Rome, on the Sacred Way that ran along the edge of the Forum. This was the heart of the trade in the city—there are similar inscriptions of no fewer than six other *margaritarii* who were based there—and on our first morning in Rome we had undoubtedly walked past the site where he had done business, as we followed the Sacred Way to Marina Piranomonte's office. The trade demanded a certain amount of capital, and Euhodus had probably done well. After all, he had put by enough to pay for his monument and its well-cut inscription in iambic verse. And he had not only owned slaves but had enough freedmen to distinguish in his will between those whose bones and ashes he permitted to join his own and those he did not.

The dead man speaks self-consciously and circumspectly, with a clear sense of his audience: travelers coming from the city, as we were, with the monument on their left. He also has a clear idea of how he wants to present himself and why. Prosperous he might have been, but he calls himself *pauper*—not a "pauper" in the sense we use the word, just not very wealthy, a man of modest means by the standards of the day, when those standards were being set by the likes of Marcus Licinius Crassus. That description is in harmony with the three other traits he gives himself: "good" (*bonus*), "compassionate" (*misericors*), and "devoted" (*amans*). (The last two words of Euhodus's self-description, *amantis pauperis*, are more commonly taken to mean "loving the poor," but this meaning is wildly unlikely, both for grammatical reasons and because it imposes a Christian virtue on a man who lived in a pre-Christian world, where this virtue was not yet known.) These are just the traits that you would expect of a man with the Greek name Euhodus, which literally means "easy going" (of a road) and by extension "easygoing" (a *euhodus* god was one well-disposed to heed your prayers). So far from being an arrogant rich man, then, the sort who cares only for his own wants and so becomes an object of envy and ill will, Euhodus is a good and modest man whose attention is fixed on others and their needs. He is just the sort of man, in other words, who deserves to have his last request honored: do not mistreat this *monumentum* of mine—this means of remembrance and the memory of me it preserves. Mistreatment was a real concern, which another freedman—a fictional character this time, the wealthy and arrogant Trimalchio of Petronius's *Satyricon*—sought to address by different means: his will provided for one of his freedmen to be stationed by his tomb, "so that the people might not run up to shit on my *monumentum*."

As we looked at the inscription, a man came bounding—there's no other word for it—out of the bright light of the *campagna* on the other side of the road. Well into his sixties, balding and bare-chested, with a tee-shirt draped over his shoulders, he was beaming with delight. He had seen our interest in the inscription, correctly identified us as folks from away, and reasonably supposed that we were clueless, so he proceeded to explicate the inscription for us and translate it into Italian.

Now here I have to confess something of which I am deeply ashamed: I do not speak Italian, in fact I speak no language other than English. Given my line of work, I am in this regard very much an oddity: in a university department of fifteen members, a third of whom have English as their second, third, or even fifth language, I am one of only two monoglots. Yes, I can read academic versions of Italian and a couple of the other modern European languages, for professional reasons, just as I can read ancient Greek and Latin. I can even understand spoken Italian reasonably well, provided it is spoken slowly enough for me to picture the words in written form—hearing as another form of reading, that is to say. But those are passive uses of language. When it comes to taking the spoken language in fluently by ear and sending it back out again by mouth—let's just say I'd have to be twice as good as I am to count as poor.

So here we had the odd situation of the enthusiastic gentleman translating a text I could read into a language I couldn't speak, and doing, I'm sure, not a bad job of it. I looked hopefully toward Laura for tactful support, but she had developed a sudden and intense interest in a bed of wildflowers off by the side of the road, and I was left to my own devices.

Now it seemed that the gentleman was saying something about Caecilia Metella . . .

" . . . impudente!"

. . . of whom he evidently disapproved. I realized he must have her confused with another woman of the same name, who a generation earlier had been one of the wives of . . .

"il dittatore Sulla—uomo brutto, eh?"

. . . yes, a very bad man indeed, and . . .

"cinque spose, cinque!"

. . . not the most constant of husbands. I tried to agree, but the words now were coming too thick and fast for me to jam one of my own in edgewise. Grabbing some sounds from the air and transforming them into text in my head, I realized that we had moved beyond the old Romans to memories of the gentleman's own life. His face became increasingly animated, the color in it rose, a vein in his temple pulsed. He had . . .

" . . . università degli studi . . ."

. . . right, studied at university, then . . .

" . . . professore . . ."

. . . held a variety of jobs including—what?—teaching mathematics in Japan? Could that be right? Well, whatever it was, his vivid gestures made clear it had been an exciting time in his life, even though—his speech and gestures slowing now, his bare shoulders sagging—it came with a heavy cost.

"Mi sposa," he sighed. His wife had stayed behind in Italy with their son, but by the time he returned, she had left him, taking the boy with her.

And there was still worse:

"Mama . . ."

His mother, his dear mother, had pined for him, longed for him, and finally died of grief while he was gone, leaving him, his expression made plain, still shadowed by the loss. The waves of remembrance washed over him and, however imperfectly grasped, over me as well, until he was done and, with a smile and good wishes, was gone, bounding off again past Euhodus's tomb into the *campagna* beyond. What a strange intersection, I thought, of memories past and present, as though the *monumentum* that gave a glimpse into the life of an ancient pearl dealer had somehow moved this man to share his own remembrances with passing travelers. "Stop, stranger . . ."

We walked farther out on the road and, because that day was our last on the Appia near Rome, we talked about what we would do tomorrow. As we turned and started back toward the city, we saw four people striding vigorously toward us, as plainly American in their dress and bearing as we were. As we closed the gap between us, one of them—obviously pegging us as we had pegged them—called out, "How far's Rome?" The way you're heading? About 25,000 miles, I thought but did not say. It emerged that they were a family traveling together, the mother and father from Houston, with two sons in their late twenties now launched and scattered to other parts. After a couple of days in Rome they had run out of things to do (well, to be fair, it was a Monday, and the museums were closed . . .), and so they had decided to spend the day on the Appian Way, taking the metro and bus to the Cecilia Metella stop as we had done, then walking back to the city. Except that they had got turned around and walked miles and miles in the wrong direction. As they started back with us, we chatted for a bit and compared notes ("I guess we'll end up in your book, eh?," one of the sons said), then they accelerated to resume their vigorous pace and make up the lost time. As they pulled away, I heard the other son say, "Well, it looks like not all roads lead to Rome."

Oh yes they do—if you choose the right way to go. And given the choice we had made about what to do next, I was happy to take that random comment, Roman style, as an excellent omen.

II
GHOST·ROAD

Italy and the Appian Way

Since we were in Rome, it was the obvious thing to hop in a rental car and set out for the south from there. But an unusual attack of good sense had warned me off. My view of the Appia was already Rome-centered enough, just by virtue of my profession. Working our way out from the capital would only prolong and confirm that view: hail the conquering power, muscling its way down the peninsula.

Now it was time, we decided, to put ourselves in the shoes of someone coming to Rome from the other end. So instead of a car we hopped a morning train, heading not south at first but north by northeast, over and through the Apennines to Ancona on the Adriatic coast. A change of trains, and it was a straight shot down the coastal plain, through the Marche, Abruzzo, and Molise into Puglia. We pulled into the port city of Brindisi (Brundisium)* with the sun already low in the sky, and by the time we had sorted out our hotel and walked to the harbor, it was dusk.

THE END OF THE ROADS

In fact, there was a time not so long ago when strolling to the harbor of Brindisi at dusk would have been a borderline-crazy thing to do. It was a town you passed through only to catch a ferry heading east, or to disembark on your return, and not at all a nice place. The

*In this essay I use a city's modern name in the text; once again, the corresponding Latin name appears in parentheses the first time the city is mentioned.

streets were filthy, the piazzas were strewn with backpackers waiting for their boats, and in the town's shadows pickpockets and thugs
waited to prey on the backpackers. All that has changed dramatically in the last decade, starting with the local authorities' decision
to move the ferry terminals from the center of the city to a spot two
miles out of town. The move coincided with an economic boom,
and the boom led to a thorough urban facelift, including the trans-
formation of the city's broad central avenue into a pedestrian mall
paved with smooth blonde stone. Now the stone gleams under the
streetlights, a yellow brick road leading down to the sea.

The sky to the east was a deep, cloudy lavender, and the bats were
starting to flit about as we stood looking out over the harbor at the
base of one of the columns that marked the Appia's end. Two columns originally stood here, put up around 200 CE as navigational
aids for ships coming in from the sea, but only the base of the second remains: that column's other drums were given centuries ago to
the city of Lecce (ancient Lupiae), twenty-five miles farther down Italy's heel, where they were reassembled and raised to support a statue
of the city's patron, Sant' Oronzo, who was believed to have freed
Brindisi from a plague. As a long list of conquerors could testify—
besides the Romans, there have been the Ostrogoths, the Byzantine
Empire (twice), the Lombards, the Saracens, the Normans, Vene-
tians, and the Kingdom of Naples in its various guises—the city is
well worth controlling, for it has one of the great natural harbors in
Italy. A returning ship passed through the broad and well-protected
mouth that opens on the Adriatic and entered a narrow throat directly across from the columns. Once through the throat, the ship
could choose between two sheltered anchorages that branch off to
either side. That branching gave the town its name—Brentēsion
in Greek, from the word meaning "stag's head" (*brention*) in Mes-
sapic, the native language of the region. And it was mimicked in the
branching roads that, depending on your point of view, ended or began here.

For in fact there was not one Appian Way but two, and they pre-

Figure 11. Pillars at the Appia's end, Brindisi (*left*) and Lecce (*right*)

sented the traveler with a choice. There was the Appia that we've been talking about all along—the real Appia, as I think of it—and then there was the via Appia Traiana, an alternate route between Brindisi and Benevento (Beneventum) that the emperor Trajan built early in the second century CE, largely on the remains of an older road, the via Minucia. We'll talk in a bit about the differences between the two, but the fundamental point in either case is this: whichever choice they make, modern travelers are chasing a ghost. This is not anything like Rome, where substantial tracts of the basalt stones have been recovered and where—even if the stones are gone—you know you're following the original roadbed. In the south, the ancient roadway is for all practical purposes gone, destroyed by wave after wave of invaders and pillagers, or simply buried by neglect and the irresistible encroachments of nature.

The towns and cities that the roads originally fostered mostly remain, in one form or another, but the cords of pavement that linked them like pearls on a string have vanished, except for the rare surfacing of a patch here and there, or the remains of an ancient bridge. The scene we found at Aeclanum, near Mirabella Eclano about fifteen miles southwest of Benevento, is typical. A town of the Samnites and then a Roman colony, Aeclanum is the modest sort of country place that the Appia connected with a larger world. It has remains of the baths and amphitheater that any self-respecting Roman town would have wanted. And it produced two notable sons—Velleius Paterculus, one of Rome's lesser historians (first century CE), and the bishop Julian, a vigorous theological opponent of Saint Augustine (fifth century CE)—before a Byzantine army destroyed it in 663. The baths and amphitheater, along with some streets and other buildings, have been excavated, and they're worth the modest fee that's charged for a visit. But when we asked where the via Appia was, the site's superintendent pointed to a spot about forty feet beyond the excavations, in a field covered with knee-high grass, and indicated that the road itself was perhaps ten feet under ground. That seemed about right: a yard or so for every five hundred years.

So it's a fair question to ask: how do we know where the ancient roads went? The honest answer is: in most places we don't know exactly where they went, and in some places we can venture only a very general estimate. A sheep track here and there can give a clue, or a modern road can be taken to approximate the route of the ancient road. (SS7, a good secondary road that runs south from Rome, makes a fair claim to do just that for the Appia.) But of the sequences that the ancient roads followed—from town to resting station to the next town—there can be no doubt, because of resources that have come down to us from ancient times.

The most extraordinary of these is the *Tabula Peutingeriana* (roughly, "Peutinger's Painted Panel"), a series of twelve parchment

Figure 12. Via Appia, Aeclanum

leaves (one now lost) that when joined together as a roll formed a painted map twenty-two feet long and just over a foot wide representing the public roadways of the Roman world, from southeast England to the tip of the Indian subcontinent. Known by the name of the German politician and diplomat who came to possess it in 1508 (Konrad Peutinger, 1465–1547), the roll was produced in 1265 by a monk at Colmar in Alsace, and it is clear that he was working from a model with a very ancient pedigree. With few exceptions, the map contains no features more recent than about the year 300, and there is reason to think that the original version, on which the monk's model in turn was based, was at least a hundred years older still. Though it has features that look modern—the land painted a light beige, the sea greenish-blue, the roads drawn in red—the map does not pretend to represent the world drawn to scale with geographic accuracy. Its purpose is rather to show the towns and resting places that the roads joined, with the distances written in Roman numerals denoting the Roman miles from point to point.

In other words, the *Tabula* is a pictorial version of one of the itineraries, or mileage tables, that have also come down to us from antiquity. The "Itinerary of Antoninus Augustus," for example, dates to the early third century and traces the distances traveled on over 250 different routes in the Empire, while the "Itinerary of Bordeaux" was produced in the fourth century for pilgrims traveling from western Gaul to Jerusalem. These compilations simply listed the places in sequence and the mileage between them, in a completely formulaic way—boring as reading material, but effective.

If you wanted to consult an itinerary in planning a journey from Brindisi to Benevento by the via Appia Traiana, you would find something like this:*

---

*Here and on the similar tables below, the distances given in Roman miles on the ancient itineraries have been converted to statute miles, which are slightly longer. The phrases in quotation marks translate the Latin names of way stations; the names of towns are in bold.

Brindisi to Benevento through Troia (Aecae), 193 miles

"At the Caves"	17 miles
"At the Tenth Mile"	9 miles
Egnazia (Egnatia/Gnathia)	10 miles
"Aurelian Towers"	15 miles
"Julian Towers"	9 miles
Bari (Barium)	10 miles
Bitonto (Butuntum)	11 miles
Ruvo di Puglia (Rubi)	10 miles
"At the Fifteenth Mile"	10 miles
Canosa di Puglia (Canusium)	14 miles
"At the Eleventh Mile"	10 miles
Ordona (Herdoniae/civitas Serdonis)	14 miles
Troia (Aecae)	17 miles
"Rest Station of Aquilo"	9 miles
"Rest Station at Aequum Tuticum/Equus Tuticus"	8 miles
"The Border of Apulia and Campania"	
"Rest Station at Forum Novum"	11 miles
Benevento (Beneventum)	9 miles

A glance at the itinerary with a modern topographical map in hand quickly reveals the attractions of the Traiana for a traveler: there are very few steep climbs. Between the ports of Brindisi and Bari the road ran at sea level, hugging the coast. Even when it turned inland at Bari, the terrain presented no challenges, just gently undulating hills the whole way, at elevations generally under five hundred feet. The road passed through higher terrain for only about thirty-five miles, from just before Troia to just after the rest station at Forum Novum, and in that stretch it climbed to more than two thousand feet for only about nine miles—very different, as we'll see, from the course of the original Appia.

The generally friendly terrain explains why the Traiana, though not much shorter in mileage, was significantly quicker, saving the traveler a full day or more between Brindisi and Benevento. For visual variety it's the more boring route, it must be said, but given the difficulties of ancient travel, boring was good. No wonder that when the poet Horace traveled from Rome to Brindisi in 37 BCE, his party denied themselves the pleasure of taking the old Appia from Benevento—and of giving Horace a chance to see his hometown, Venosa (Venusia)—and instead chose to travel on the Traiana's predecessor, the via Minucia. As Horace records in his poem about the trip (*Satires* 1.5), the leg from Benevento to Brindisi took the group five days—at a bit under forty modern miles a day, a pace at the high end of normal, or even a bit better.

A day's travel was not expected to take you very far very fast, and another glance at the itinerary shows the accommodations that were made to this fact. Between the towns and the various kinds of rest stations—a "changing place" (*mutatio*) where you could get fresh animals to pull or carry you, or a "stopping place" (*mansio, statio*) where you could spend the night—you needn't go very far before pausing to regroup somewhere other than in the middle of the open countryside: just over eleven miles on average, with a segment as long as sixteen or seventeen miles very much the exception.

This was a blessing, because travel by land was very hard, as it was everywhere and at all times before the coming of the railroad in the nineteenth century. You could walk or you could ride, but either way the pace was not going to be dramatically different, unless you were (say) Julius Caesar rushing to reach your army in Gaul, with a string of fast and strong horses at your disposal. (In 58 BCE Caesar covered the eight hundred miles between Rome and Gaul, over the Alps, in eight days.)* If you were going to ride, then you had to choose your means of conveyance: man or beast? The human option pointed you toward a sedan chair, the limousine of antiquity, reserved for the elite.

---

*Not bad, but couriers using the Royal Road of the Persian Empire could cover more than 1,500 miles, between Sardis (modern Sart, in western Turkey) and Susa (modern Shush, in western Iran), in nine days.

These were generally for shorter trips, but the long haul was not un-heard of: a married couple would have his and hers chairs, and of course your status would be reflected in the number of slaves carrying each chair.

But the more common alternative was the horse (for riding) or the mule (for pulling), and the more common of these two was the mule. One or another variety of wagon, covered or more usually open, was the chief vehicle, with one or more mules to provide the locomotion and a muleteer to keep the animals moving. Then one last thing to decide: having opted for the mule-drawn wagon, you had to settle on the number of wagons that you would use. For of course you were not going to be traveling alone, especially if you were a person of quality. You would have slaves to handle your baggage and chamber pots, and just to demonstrate how important you were: an entourage of thirty would not be exceptional. Oh, and the weapons: you and at least some of your slaves were going to be armed, because banditry—the guerrilla warfare waged by the peasantry against unwary folk from the cities—was a chronic problem, and no sane person traveled through the open countryside unarmed or unprotected by armed companions.

So you settled into the wagon—if "settle" is the verb you want to use, the way the planks were already raising welts—and tried to ignore the stink of the mules. You counted the heads of your entourage, to make sure they were all present and accounted for. Perhaps you recalled how Spartacus provided his army of the enslaved with weapons taken from travelers, and you ran your hand nervously over the hilt of your own sword.

Right, then: ready to set out for the north on the older, longer Appia.

THE LAYERS OF THE LAND

Like most Americans who travel to Italy, we had kept to a handful of predictable patches on our earlier trips—Rome, Tuscany, the Veneto, the sliver of Campania around the Bay of Naples, the Amalfi coast—and we didn't know what to expect in the south, beyond the fact that—culturally, historically—it most definitely wasn't the north. Take the Renaissance, for example. That great welling up of genius to which names like Leonardo, Michelangelo, and Botticelli are attached is all but synonymous with Italy in the American mind—and yet where southern Italy is concerned, the Renaissance simply did not happen. What we know as the Renaissance emerged from the mercantile and banking centers of the north; southern Italy—the Kingdom of Naples—was held by a succession of foreign dynasties that mostly viewed the region as a place from which to extract as much wealth as possible. The resulting economic and cultural backwardness accounts in part for the contempt in which the north has held the south, captured in the astounding maxim, "Africa begins in Rome."

So the parts of Italy traversed by the Appia south of Rome were terra incognita for us, and that was one of the trip's great attractions. Wanting to take in as much of it as possible in first impressions when I was there on the ground, I limited the advance reading I did and had only a very general idea what to expect. I was certainly unprepared for the wonderful variety of the landscapes that we found, and the many places of great beauty. At the same time, we were reminded at virtually every stop of how land and culture interact, and how following the Appia brings past and present together in multiple layers. Discovering those layers was the point of the trip, and while some discoveries were obvious and inevitable, others—the most surprising or revealing, it turned out—were the result of mere chance.

The account that follows will take us through the journey from Brindisi to the outskirts of Rome in five segments that blend the physical encounter and visual experience with the discovery of cultural and historical layers we met as we chased the Appia's ghost. At the head of each segment I'll set out the itinerary, like the itinerary for the via Appia Traiana that we saw earlier; the distances again are in statute miles, while names in square brackets belong to ancient towns that have no surely identifiable modern counterpart.

Brindisi to Taranto, 40 miles

"Scamnum"	15 miles
Oria (Uria)	7 miles
"Mesochorum"	9 miles
Taranto (Taras/Tarentum)	9 miles

From one great harbor to another, the road runs mostly straight and mostly flat across the heel of Italy's boot, passing through some of the peninsula's most featureless terrain. Much of southern Italy had already been deforested in antiquity to make way for *latifundia*, vast estates formed from the aggregation of many smallholdings and then farmed by armies of slaves to grow the staples of the ancient diet—olives, grapes, and grains. (The elder Pliny, a believer in the old ways, thought it wise "to sow less land and plow it better" and declared, "The *latifundia* have ruined Italy.") The *latifundia* find their latter-day reflection in the haciendas that sprang up in South America starting in the early sixteenth century, when huge tracts of land were granted to conquistadors, and in the nearly simultaneous rise of the *masserie*, fortified centers of production scattered throughout southern Italy and Sicily. The Spanish played a part here too, for they then controlled the south through the Kingdom of Sicily and the Kingdom of Naples and distributed these baronial estates with the intent of reclaiming for agriculture land that had been abandoned. The *masserie*—some of them now adapted to the ways of agritourism—are still a dominant feature of the southern Italian countryside, and the territory between Brindisi and Taranto is no exception.

As you move along, flat vistas extending to the horizon alternate with old and beautiful olive groves that line the road to produce a tunnel-like focus. The land rises to elevations over two hundred fifty feet, where you can spy the polychrome dome of the basilica of Oria, a modest town atop a modest hill about halfway between the coasts. Besides a castle dating to the thirteenth century and the baroque cathedral dating to the eighteenth, Oria can also claim one of the oldest Jewish communities in Europe, with roots probably going back to classical times. (The Jewish quarter is marked by a wooden sign on a base like a hat rack: since the sign is obviously moveable, and since the area it marks is absolutely indistinguishable from any other amid the old town's twisting streets, I developed the nutty conviction that the locals shift the sign around from day to day, as a joke on visitors.) The land rises so gradually as you move inland from Brindisi that the descent toward Taranto comes as a surprise. Surely you've been at sea-level all along, you think, only to find a lower plateau spreading open before you, and another beyond that, one great plane tipping out onto the next, down to the sea.

Ancient Taras began as Sparta's only colony, set on a splendid crescent of a bay, in the late eighth century BCE, and by the time the Roman conquest changed its name to Tarentum five centuries later, it was the most powerful, wealthy, and culturally advanced city between the Greek mainland and Syracuse in Sicily. You would guess none of this from looking at modern Taranto. Substantial building that began in the eighteenth century had become a mania by the late nineteenth century, leaving very little that was ancient still visible. The heavy bombardment the city suffered in 1940, when the Royal Air Force attacked the Italian naval base there, did nothing to help matters. And industrial development since the end of the war has made Taranto the most polluted city in western Europe, with staggering levels of carbon monoxide, carbon dioxide, and dioxin. This is a city, in short, that you think you'll want to see in your rearview mirror as soon as possible. But then you enter the archaeological museum—a stunning jewel set in an undistinguished older building— and you say, "Oh!"

You find case upon case in room after room of the most exquisite Greek art that I have seen outside Athens, dating from long before the Romans' arrival: crowns and necklaces of delicate gold leaf, cunningly worked figurines, elegant red-figure vases, and much more. Interesting, you think. It's one thing to know, say, that one of the city's sons, Archytas of Tarentum, a friend of Plato and seven times his homeland's general, was a major philosopher and mathematician in the first half of the fourth century BCE, well before the Appia was a gleam in anyone's eye. It's quite another to see in three dimensions the evidence of the culture—more sophisticated than Rome's—that the Appia encountered when it reached Tarentum a century or so later. Where else, you wonder, will you see evidence like this?

Taranto to Venosa, 87 miles

"Canales"	18 miles
"Sublupatia"	12 miles
[Blera]	13 miles
Gravina di Puglia (Silvium)	26 miles
Venosa (Venusia)	18 miles

The terrain rises again, as you come out of Taranto and head northwest, first toward Castellaneta, a prosperous-looking town once "The Home of Rudolf Valentino" (so say the signs), and then on toward Gravina. The rise is gradual at first, then accelerates, and before long you're at elevations over a thousand feet. This is the western edge of Le Murge, the rectangular plateau of more than 1,500 square miles that dominates the topography of Puglia, starting just north of the passage between Brindisi and Taranto and running parallel with the coast, southeast to northwest. "Le Murge" is grammatically plural, referring both to the lower-lying Bassa Murgia, where the land is more fertile, and to the higher Alta Murgia. Here the terrain makes you believe the supposed derivation of *murgia* from the Latin word *murex*, "sharp stone."

Gravina, which the ancient Appia knew as Silvium, sits at the edge of the Alta Murgia National Park, in a landscape rife with caverns, sinkholes, ravines, and gorges formed by acidic water acting on the region's limestone bedrock. The town is a severe beauty, built up to the rim of a deep gorge that runs along its western edge. The gorge plunges a hundred fifty feet to the stream that formed it ages ago,

Figure 13. Gravina

and in late spring its gray rock face peeks out from behind a mask of deep green shrubs and grasses dotted with wildflowers. As the rock descends, cypresses rise thirty feet or more from shallow roots, exclamation points delighted that they should be springing up while everything around them is falling down. Caves and chapels are cut into the stone on one side of the ravine, and the modern city looms on the other, the two joined by an ancient stone bridge and viaduct.

Arriving when we did, we learned that we had just missed the Fiera San Giorgio, one of the oldest agricultural fairs in Europe, which has been held in Gravina in the latter part of April for over seven hundred years. So we consoled ourselves with a good lunch and a tale of three churches.

The most unmistakable and unavoidable church in Gravina is of course the cathedral, which presides over the gorge. The cathedral is the heart of any Italian town large enough to merit a bishop: the bishopric of Gravina dates to the ninth century. When the Normans, led by the Hauteville brothers, took Sicily and all of southern Italy in the eleventh century, they took Gravina, too, and made it the seat of a count in the Kingdom of Sicily. By the end of that century the town sported a proper castle and a proper Romanesque cathedral, built so that its walls were continuous with the castle's walls.

There the cathedral stood for nearly 400 years, as the Kingdom of Sicily (later, the Kingdom of Naples) passed from Norman hands to German hands (the Hohenstaufens), then to French hands (the Angevins), then to Spanish hands (the Aragonese). Then the cathedral fell, not because of political upheaval but because of upheavals of a different sort: after a fire did serious damage in 1447, a massive earthquake brought the cathedral down just before Christmas in 1456.

Thirty years passed before the building that stands today was raised on the ruins of the old, under the leadership of the bishop and the most prominent local families, chief among them the Orsini, who have been the lords of Gravina since 1417: the twenty-second Orsini to be Duke of Gravina, Domenico Napoleone II Orsini, lives today in Rome. This cathedral looks to be built for eternity. Its flanks, massive and even forbidding, rise up in two stories of blank stone blocks broken only occasionally by narrow slits of windows. Inside, though, it's a pleasant structure, lighter and airier than the outside leads you to expect. Fourteen columns separated by rounded arches divide the inner space into three aisles, in typical basilica fashion, and a rose window with twenty-four rays, among the largest in southern Italy, looks out over the main portal. A carved and gilded wood ceiling was added in the seventeenth century, a grand organ somewhat later. It's a cathedral any town could be proud of.

Now, a story like this could probably be told, with different actors in different settings at different times, about most of the cathedrals of Italy, just because such churches have been central to the spiritual and political life of cities and towns from one end of the peninsula to the other since the early Middle Ages. And that is the main reason I have told it, so that its typicality, its almost generic character, could stand as a contrast to the stories I have to tell about two other churches in Gravina that are more distinctive of their time and place.

As we followed the cobbled streets away from the gorge and the cathedral back toward the center of town, we soon came to another church, whose façade of white stone blocks was blazing in the afternoon heat, and whose plain wood doors, painted a flat, pale green, were surrounded by a striking portal. This is the church of Santa Maria del Suffragio. It was built in 1649 with funds provided by Ferdinando III Orsini, Duke of Gravina, and his wife, Giovanna Frangipani della Tolfa, and it's the Orsini coat of arms that the impressive skeletons frame above the lintel. As the parents of the future Pope Benedict XIII, the third and last Orsini to reach the See of St. Peter, the duke and duchess were appropriately pious—in fact, their funding of the church might be linked to the birth of their son in February of the same year. In any event, their piety took shape in a way that unmistakably joined in a contemporary Christian controversy.

The Italian word *suffragio* descends directly from the Latin *suffragium*, a word that originally meant "vote," as its English offspring, "suffrage," would lead you to expect. But in a way that says a lot about Roman political history, and Rome's passage from a semidemocratic Republic to an autocratic Empire, the common meaning of *suffragium* changed from "vote" to "patronage" or "intercession," the protection of the lowly by the great. "Intercession" is just what is at issue here. The church was dedicated to the celebration of masses for the repose of the souls of the dead in purgatory through the intercession of the Blessed Virgin Mary, like the church of Santa Maria delle Anime del Purgatorio—"of the souls in purgatory"—built thirty years earlier in Naples, or the church of the Mother of God Who Consoles the Afflicted built twenty years later in Bitonto, on the via Appia Traiana, with a searing image of purgatory above its portal.

So Santa Maria del Suffragio was a *chiesa del purgatorio*, a "purgatory church," of the sort that sprang up all over southern Italy and Sicily—and only in southern Italy and Sicily—from the middle of the sixteenth through the seventeenth century. The impulse to build

Figure 14. Purgatory church, Gravina

Figure 15. Purgatory church, Bitonto

them arose in reaction to the Protestant Reformation, as a token of the Catholic Counter-Reformation, launched by the church at the Council of Trent held between 1545 and 1563.

According to Catholic doctrine, purgatory is literally a "place of cleansing," where souls suffer for a time because of the forgivable sins that, unfortunately, God had not yet forgiven at the time of death. The suffering is as intense as the pains the damned know in Hell, but it is not eternal. The length of one's stay depends on the nature and number of the sins, and it can be shortened both by the sinner's acts of penance while still alive and by the prayers and other pious acts— pilgrimages, say, or fasts—performed by the living for the benefit of the deceased: hence the priest's injunction that I recall from my Catholic boyhood, to "pray for the souls of the faithful departed," a call clearly intended to benefit neither the departed in Heaven, who need no prayers, nor the departed in Hell, who are beyond the reach of prayer.

We can already recognize a purgatorial doctrine in some pre-

Christian thinking on the afterlife, for example in the passage of Vergil's *Aeneid* that describes how souls, before they can be released to the Elysian Fields, must be cleansed of the "plagues of the body" that stained them in life, some souls even being hung out to dry like laundry on a line. One big problem, however, according to the Protestant point of view, is that the doctrine is not recognizable in Christian scripture: or as Article 22 of the Church of England puts it, it is "a fond thing vainly invented and grounded upon no warranty of scripture, but rather repugnant to the Word of God." The other big problem for the Protestants was the sale of "indulgences." Starting from the premise that the pious acts of the living could cause a certain amount of the deceased's punishment in purgatory to be remitted (Latin *indulgentia* could denote the annulment of a penal sentence), and aided by the further premise that the church itself could directly grant remissions in response to those who prayed or fasted, the custom arose of accepting cash in lieu of pious acts, a practice the Protestants found corrupt and repulsive. But the Council of Trent, at its twenty-fifth and last meeting, reaffirmed the doctrine of purgatory and the efficacy of indulgences, while banning their sale. The purgatory churches of south Italy gave substance, very emphatically, to that reaffirmation.

But the purgatory churches were not dedicated only to the relief of those already paying for their sins in the next life. That's where those impressive skeletons come in. Like the church in Gravina, like the church in Bitonto, like the church in Terracina that borders the Appia as it passes through the town's center, many of the purgatory churches have prominent representations of death among their decorative elements both inside and outside. Skeletons and death's heads abound, often accompanied by messages that float alongside them like the dialogue balloons in a cartoon: "Hodie mihi, cras tibi," one skeleton says about the coming of death—"Today for me, tomorrow for you"; "Quod es, fui, quod sum, eris," another offers—"What you are, I was, what I am, you will be." Which is to say, "Memento mori," a phrase that combines a command (*memento* = "remember /

Figure 16. Purgatory church, Terracina

be mindful") and an action (*mori* = "die"): not "Remember to die"—as though it were an item on a particularly grim to-do list—but "Be mindful that you *are* dying." As we live, we die, coming ever closer, inexorably, to the day when we will have to give an accounting and pay for our unforgiven sins. As calls for reform and penance, the skeletons symbolize the second half of a purgatory church's mission: not just to seek the repose of the souls of the faithful departed already in purgatory, but to help the faithful still among the living keep from joining their number.

The purgatory church was a distinctive emblem of southern Italian Christianity, but we didn't want to leave Gravina without seeing one of the other churches still more specific to the landscape the Appia crossed, the *chiese rupestri*, or "rock churches." As their name suggests, these are churches whose makers took advantage of the region's karst topography by carving them out of the living stone: there are nearly two hundred of them in Matera, to the east and south of Gravina, and nearly twice that number have been catalogued in Puglia and Basilicata together. But we were stumped. The oldest and grandest—the church of San Michele delle Grotte, dating to around 1000 and dedicated to Gravina's patron saint, the Archangel—was not open to the public, and we simply could not find the handful of others that we knew were somewhere around. We followed the narrow, winding street as it made its way, one switchback at a time, down the Fondovico district that extends to the base of the gorge, and then followed it back up again—nothing. At street level a final moment of frustration brought us face to face with what appeared to be a small bell tower, with a wooden plaque affixed to it, announcing the church of Saint Basil the Great, of the twelfth to thirteenth century. Terrific! But where?

Just then we spied a young man with a bag of groceries getting out of a late-model BMW parked nearby. A native who knew the area, I figured, so I attempted, "Mi scusi, signore, dove sono le chiese rupestri?" He paused for a moment—evidently trying to decide if what I'd said could really have been Italian—then gestured for us to wait while he walked to the house next to the bell tower. Opening the door, he called out, "Mama! Mama!," followed by a few quick comments I didn't catch, and within seconds Mama had emerged, broad as she was tall and carrying a set of keys. She unlocked a gate, motioned for us to follow, then hurried—I mean, absolutely bounced—down a short flight of stairs, at the base of which she unlocked another gate and threw it open.

There, under the contemporary, middle-class house, was a complete gem of a tiny church, on the order of eight hundred years old. Eight columns, forming three short aisles, were carved from limestone that ranged from white to soft gold. The single altar was carved from the same rock, as were all the decorative moldings on the walls. The floor tiles were a subdued rose and white. And the altar piece—the Virgin and child, flanked by Saint Basil and another saint I couldn't identify—was brilliantly colored, with crisp green, red, blue, and gold. As we oohed and aahed and walked through the

Figure 17. Church of Saint Basil the Great, Gravina

church, Mama beamed and seemed about to burst with proprietary pride. When we were ready to leave, she asked us to sign the guest book and seemed as grateful to have been given the chance to offer this bit of hospitality as we were grateful for receiving it.

Still, it was in Venosa, our next stop on the road to Rome, that we came upon the best church, the church, we agreed, where we felt the greatest sense of peace, and discovered some of the most interesting layers in our search.

Between Gravina and Venosa the ancient Appia wove its way along and across what is now the boundary between two administrative regions, Puglia and Basilicata. But the land cares nothing for administrative boundaries, and the plateau just rolls along on both sides of the imaginary line, as hills gently unfurl their rippling bulk eastward to the sea. It was full spring now, and all around there were intense greens of many shades—vineyards, olive groves, and open fields—and blankets of yellow flowers. The colors would have been brilliant even under a bleaching midday sun, but as we drove, a wild storm happened to blow in from Bari, on the Adriatic forty miles to the east, and the light that still came slantwise from the west caught and saturated the greens and yellows against the storm's midnight-blue backdrop. The clouds dove in, low and very fast, dark and roiling. I was reminded of the feeling I've sometimes had on the sea, the sudden dread of riding on the back of an incomprehensibly powerful beast to whom I meant nothing, save that now the beast wasn't under me but looming above. How puny and exposed must an ancient traveler have felt, if the sturdy envelope of our Fiat left me feeling so vulnerable? I confess it was a relief to put the day's driving behind us when—after a detour or two around washed-out roads—we reached old Horace's *patria*.

Like Gravina, the modern town of Venosa bears the stamp of the Orsini, who came to possess it. One of them, Count Pirro del Balzo Orsini, built both the castle and the cathedral that dominate the town's center, at about the same time that his kinsman was building

Figure 18. Between Gravina and Venosa

the church of Santa Maria del Suffragio in Gravina; and, inevitably, Venosa has a *chiesa del purgatorio* of its own.

Ancient Venusia had been a Roman colony and an important strategic outpost for over two centuries by the time Horace was born there in 65 BCE. Its old and prosperous ways continued for at least five centuries more, when it served as an important commercial hub between Apulia, Lucania (the region now called Basilicata), and Campania. The Jewish catacombs in the town contained the remains of wool merchants who plied their trade in this land of sheep and goats through the fourth and fifth centuries, until the Lombards swooped down in the sixth. The visible remains of the ancient town lie on the northeast edge of the modern one, where today's signs of urban life start to fade away and the countryside begins. The ruins, where the Appia must have passed, are extensive: baths, of course; an amphitheater; a temple of Hymen, the god of marriage;

houses; and the remains of the city walls. Across the modern road from the amphitheater is the abbey church of the Santissima Trinità, built in the middle of the eleventh century from the stones of the amphitheater, on the site of an earlier church that had itself been built over the temple of Hymen. (For an excellent bird's-eye view, go to 40°58′08.14″N, 15°49′38.82″E on Google Earth.) So here Romanesque stands cheek by jowl with Roman.

The church survives thanks to the failure of another, larger ecclesiastical project begun a century later. The Benedictine monks who had a chapter in Venosa planned a grand basilica on the same northwest-to-southeast axis. They got as far raising the walls, which incorporated the walls of the existing church and then continued on beyond them, roughly doubling their length: the rounded shell of the apse-to-be is there, the transept that would have passed before the altar, even the columns that would have supported the vaulting and defined the aisle on the basilica's south side. But that is all: construction simply stopped, leaving the new work open to the heavens and the older church embedded in the skeleton of the new.

On the day we found the church, the after-effects of the storm that had swept over us on the road from Gravina were still in the air. The overcast sky spat rain fitfully, the thick grass soaked our shoes as we tromped along the old walls, and by the time we approached the front of the church a chill that had replaced the springtime heat was making us shiver. The façade itself could not have been simpler, with a plain wooden door framed by two stone lions, and the entry was exceedingly dark. But then, when we entered the nave itself, the space exploded with light, even on that overcast day.

Areas in the floor have been cut out, with thick acrylic plastic put in place of the stone, exposing the Roman mosaic surfaces beneath. From the walls, fourteenth-century frescoes look down upon the ancient mosaics, and in the heart of the church are two eleventh-century tombs. One belongs to Alberada, first wife of Robert II Guiscard, who succeeded his brother Humphrey as Duke of Apulia and Calabria from 1059 to 1085. The second tomb, on the wall opposite, contains the bones of Robert and Humphrey themselves, along with those of William Iron-Arm and Drogo. These are the four Hauteville brothers who had led their Norman forces through southern Italy and Sicily, conquering as they went, establishing a dynasty that determined the history of the region for a century and a half and setting the foundations for the Kingdom of Sicily—but here they lay in a tomb of stunning simplicity, an unadorned stone sarcophagus under a fresco of the Crucifixion framed by two brick columns and a pediment.

And then, as I said, there is the light. In the wall of the apse that looks out on the unfinished basilica beyond, a series of tall, arched windows are cut—whether as part of the original design or as a more recent innovation, I could not get close enough to tell—and through them the light pours over the altar, as though the basilica's skeletal walls were funneling it in. The church seems a bright stage on which a dance of history mingles ancient and medieval, Hymen and Hauteville. But it is also a great deal more than that, a place so serene and fine that we wanted to stay and breathe in the peace, at the same time that we felt ourselves to be intruding in a spiritual world where we had no rightful place.

Venosa to Benevento, 75 miles

"Pons Aufidi"	22 miles
Lacedonia (Aquilonia)	10 miles
"Sub Romula"	10 miles
Mirabella Eclano (Aeclanum)	19 miles
"Ad Calorem"	5 miles
Benevento (Beneventum)	9 miles

What happened next was one of the discoveries we owed to chance—though Laura might prefer to insert "Bob's pigheadedness" in place of "chance." (Actually, to say that Laura is tolerant of my quirks would be to sell her short. I, for one, would find me willful, if I had to deal with me on a daily basis, but for over forty years now Laura has wholeheartedly embraced the old proverb, when you buy a horse, you buy both ends. Certainly on these travels she served as a spirited Muse and helpful interrogator, while paying minimal attention to the less-attractive end.) I wanted to see the statue of Horace before we left Venosa, so we drove to the square in the center of town where it had been raised in 1898. That didn't take long. It's a kitschy affair, representing a man who (we happen to know) was short and chubby as a willowy youth in a toga, crowned with laurel and holding a scroll. Definitely not worth the trip.

So I punched the address for our next leg into the GPS, and we set out. The machine's robotic voice began to lead us through the *centro storico*'s cobbled, one-way streets, which seemed to become narrower with each turn. As the GPS droned on, the human dialogue in the car went like this:

"Sweetie, don't you think you should try to find another way?"

"I can make it."

"Rob, I mean it, this really doesn't look good."

"I can make it."

"Robert, PLEASE don't try this." (Hmmm—from Sweetie to Rob to Robert in nothing flat: perhaps this *is* serious.)

"I can—" WHAM!

We stopped with a jolt as the Fiat's right front wheel attempted to occupy the same space as the front steps of one of the houses that lined the street. Or perhaps more accurately, that lined the alley: the road, we now saw, was so narrow that we could lean out the windows and touch the wall on each side. This was a spoke in the wheel of progress, for sure: we plainly could go no farther forward, and backing up—and avoiding another set of steps—was going to be pretty awkward. Damn.

But a man appeared from one of the houses and started to gesture, giving directions for me to reverse. I put the car into gear and turned the wheel as he indicated, right and left and right again, weaving backward to avoid the house steps, one set after another. When we had backed to the nearest cross street, he jumped into the rear seat and started to give directions to take us out of the historical center and back onto navigable streets. We made a slow circuit, eventually coming back to a place parallel to the spot where the scrape had begun and our savior had emerged. He asked us to stop, hopped out, and waved his good-byes as he headed home. We called out our thanks after him and showered blessings upon his descendents. What a nice break!

Indeed: break, it turned out, was the relevant word. As soon as we left town and began to pick up speed, it became clear that something had gone wrong in a major way. The steering was loose and far from optimally responsive, and a worrisome noise was starting to come from the direction of the offended wheel. After a few miles of heavy denial I pulled over and got out to take a look. Yes, there they were: rear wheels and left front all pointing in the same direction, right front angling about 30 degrees off true. Damn.

One thing was clear: the plan to make it as far as Benevento that evening was going to be revised. But in which direction? Back to Venosa? Ahead to Melfi? I had the sense that Melfi was the bigger place (as I later learned, with a population of around 18,000 it's about half again as large as Venosa) and more likely to run to the sorts of help we'd need. So we pressed on, probably foolishly, as I worried that the damn wheel was going to come neatly off exactly in the middle of a turn on the unendingly winding road, and as the noise from the wheel gradually rose from a groan to a bellow, also unending, that announced our approach from God knows how far away and drew stares wherever we passed.

But we did limp into Melfi, and I parked the car at the first spot I found. The details of what happened next are neither here nor there, though I will say this: thank God that I had, on an impulse, opted for the insurance to cover the car, something I never do when renting in the States; thank God for American Express, whose agents handled the negotiations that would put us in another rental car the next day; and thank God for the kindness and goodwill of the people of Melfi, from the man with the tow truck who calmed us, to the policemen who reassured us as we watched the car being towed away, to the restaurateur who fed us when we were ravenous, even though the restaurant was closed for a twenty-fifth anniversary party he was throwing for his sister, to the desk clerk at the hotel we checked into, who welcomed us by saying that, yes, of course, he knew New Jersey—in fact, his wife was from Summit.

Now, beyond the fact that Melfi sits in the shadow of an extinct volcano, Monte Vulture, I knew only two things about the town: first, the Appia had not passed through or even very near it, and second, as part of the territory of Venosa it had had no significant independent history as a Roman city—and so I had planned to give it a miss. Now, willy-nilly, we had nearly a full day to make its acquaintance before we took a morning train to Potenza, the provincial capital, to claim our replacement car. And this, it turned out, was one of the lucky strokes of the trip.

Here were the layers we were looking for, in a configuration we hadn't yet encountered. Melfi might have been only an annex of Venosa in Roman times, but it was a place of real consequence both before the Romans came and after they left. From very early times the town's location had made it a natural meeting place for the peoples of central Italy. To the west and southeast there were trade routes that forged ties with Etruscan settlements in Campania, the Greek cities on the Gulf of Tarentum, and later the Lucani, a Samnite people who settled the area around Potenza. To the north, the terrain quickly descends toward the alluvial plains of the River Ofanto, putting Melfi in touch with the Dauni, the dominant Italic tribe in northern Apulia. The same centrality later made the town a strategic hub from the early Middle Ages on, often as a point of contention: first between the Lombards to the north and the Byzantines to the south, later as the place from which the Hautevilles launched their conquests, and still later as the site of the "Bloody Easter" carnage (March 1528) that saw thousands of the city's inhabitants slaughtered in a clash between the Spanish and the French. All

Figure 19. Melfi

these layers merge in the hilltop castle, which looks down on the ceramic roof tiles of the town.

Most of modern Melfi lies below the remains of the old town wall that circled the citadel near its base. Passing through one of the gates in the wall, you enter a world of medieval streets that climb in terraces up the hillside. As you walk past the houses that rest upon the terraces, the sounds of families filter through doors and windows shut tight against the heat and stray passersby. The climb becomes ever steeper, it seems, but then you mount the via Santa Croce and find the gateway of the castle dead ahead.

The castle is the legacy of Robert II Guiscard, one of the brothers buried in Venosa, who had it built after Melfi became the seat of the Duchy of Apulia in 1059. What began as a simple rectangle morphed over time into an irregular polygonal structure outfitted with eight towers, three courtyards, a moat, and a drawbridge, as a series of owners—including Emperor Frederick II of Swabia, Charles I of Anjou, and Andrea Doria, admiral of the Holy Roman Empire in the early sixteenth century—shaped it to fit their needs. It was a particular favorite of Frederick's—the man called *Stupor Mundi*, "Wonder of the World," by his contemporaries—who chose it as the platform from which to promulgate the Constitutions of Melfi (1231), the first medieval compilation of administrative law, which consolidated his expanding Holy Roman Empire. After Doria received it as a reward for his naval service in 1531, the castle remained in his family until 1952, when it was given to the state. Restoration and renovation followed, sometimes set back by the region's frequent earthquakes, until the castle was transformed into the National Archaeological Museum of Vulture and Melfi in 1976. It's in the museum where the layers crowd together, letting over twenty centuries of local culture pass in quick review.

So the Doria room on the first floor has its hunting scenes. (The family mostly used the castle during hunting season.) Nearby there's the original Norman throne room. And high in the belfry (how ever did they get it there?) is an immense sarcophagus of the second century, found in the small town of Rapolla between Venosa and Melfi: the life-size figure of a woman—head on a pillow, a delicate night-dress clinging to her hips and breasts—reclines in sleep on the lid ("Sleep, the brother of Death," Homer said). Elaborate reliefs adorn all four sides, evidence that it came to central Italy from Asia Minor. (Western sarcophagi are decorated only on the front.) The sarcophagus is clearly regarded as the jewel in the museum's crown, and it is indeed very fine. But while the museum did deliver a jolt, the sarcophagus wasn't the source.

Instead, the several floors devoted to pre-Roman finds from sites in the surrounding area were the real revelation. As in Taranto, there was case after case of extraordinary and exquisite objects, for the most part originally offered up as grave-goods for the dead, starting three centuries before Rome's incursion into the south. From the late seventh century BCE, delicate Daunian ware with geometric designs and fanciful critter-shaped decorations on the handles; from the late sixth century, a glorious bronze lion, rampant, that began its career as the decorative device on a shield; from the fifth century, a brilliant polychrome drinking cup in the shape of a horse's head, a large Attic red-figured mixing bowl, a wonderfully subtle crown of twisted gold, a full warrior's outfit, including greaves, sword, and several spears, and slender Etruscan candelabra that stand a yard tall on three claw-feet; then more red-figured ware from the fourth century, a drinking cup and another mixing bowl, this time from Apulia and Campania. Italic and Etruscan and Greek influences all together, reflecting the area's service as an archaic melting pot, and reflecting, too, the high level of material culture and affluence that the region enjoyed before the coming of Rome. This was the lesson of Taranto repeated, but with an exclamation point.

As we traveled from Venosa to Melfi and then from Melfi to beyond, we came to the part of the route that offered the biggest challenge to our ancient counterparts, whether they were travelers on foot, or a horse or mule, or the original builders. From Taranto, less than fifty feet above sea level, and on through Venosa we were on a consistent upward path: about a quarter mile in vertical elevation over the course of seventy-odd miles, a fairly gentle rise. But from Venosa on, the terrain changes dramatically, and that's where the challenge lay. The road rises and falls, roller-coaster fashion, from one hill town to another, until it climbs to Lacedonia; from there it remains at over two thousand feet for many miles, until it starts its descent toward Benevento.

Heading northwest out of Venosa, the Appia skirted Melfi and Monte Vulture on a trajectory that no modern road follows, until it reached a way station at the bridge over the River Aufidus (now the Ofanto), where it began a smooth and sinuous loop toward the southwest. The modern route takes you through Melfi, and to a surprise. As you start the climb out of Melfi—a very long, steep climb—what had been a perfectly reasonable secondary road falls into utter disrepair, as though the authorities had decided, "Well, stuff that for a lark," and just walked away. Kilometer markings cease, and in their place signs abound with urgent points to make: "Sagoma deformata!" "Frana!" "Fango!" The first of these I could handle: yes indeed, the road's contours were here and there deformed, for example where half the road—the descending lane—had simply fallen away down the hillside, or where the remaining fragment of the paved road was a good three feet higher than the dirt surface on which we were driving. But my academic Italian didn't run to "Frana!" or "Fango!," and that is probably just as well: in the circumstances, knowing that "Land-slide!" and "Mud!" were on the horizon could not have helped.

So we drove on and chose to find the silver lining. There were truly magnificent views of open country on every side. And we were clearly an object of curiosity to those we passed. Not just the old woman out walking her dog who goggled at us as though she hadn't seen a car in a generation, or the ox who showed more restrained in-terest, but also the small fox who stared at us keenly. And I could more vividly appreciate the effort entailed in forcing the Appia through such country, and in maintaining it once it was there.

When the road finally turns toward Lacedonia, the disrepair ends as suddenly as it began, and soon the climbing ends too. You move now along a high ridge, where on either side you can see a succes-sion of rolling hills with stuccoed towns set atop them, like white-caps glistening on a six-foot sea. You also see, for mile after mile, many of the turbines that have made Italy the sixth largest producer of wind power in the world. They begin in smallish clusters, then march across the ridges in ranks of seventy or more, mechanical pod-creatures out of *War of the Worlds*. It is hard not to be of two minds about them. Though they give a wide berth to towns and dwell-ings, the wind turbines are now an unavoidable feature of the land-scape, without the charm of their old Dutch forerunners, which they dwarf; they are surprisingly loud; and some of them are so close to the road that it seemed a giant blade might swing round and split the car's roof like a can-opener. On the other hand, I am writing in the summer of Deepwater Horizon. Clean, renewable energy is clean,

Figure 20. Wind farm, near Lacedonia

renewable energy, and 6.7 terawatt-hours of production—Italy's achievement in 2009, only a quarter of its ultimate goal—is not nothing.* I imagine that when the aqueducts first started their own march across the countryside, they might have seemed an aesthetic blight, too.

After the wind farms and the long, high ridge, the road gradually descends through Mirabella Eclano and hills planted with olives and fruit. Roadside signs advertising a local restaurant promise "cucina tipica irpina," a token of regional pride that looks back to the Hirpini, a Samnite people who settled these hills over twenty-four centuries ago. At the Calore River ("Ad Calorem") on Benevento's out-

*One terawatt equals 1,000,000 megawatts; the average household in the United States consumes 8.9 megawatt-hours of electricity per year.

skirts there was a way station; then, after a further descent, there's Benevento itself.

Benevento to Formia, 69.5 miles

Montesarchio (Caudium)	10.00 miles
"Ad Novas"	8.25 miles
Church of San Giacomo alle Galazze (Calatia)	5.50 miles
Santa Maria Capua Vetere (Capua)	5.50 miles
"Ad Octavum"	7.25 miles
"Pons Campanus"	8.25 miles
Mondragone (Sinuessa)	8.25 miles
Minturno (Minturnae)	8.25 miles
Formia (Formiae)	8.25 miles

At an elevation of a little over four hundred feet, Benevento lies in a bowl, with Monte Taburno to its back in the west and other highlands to the northeast and south. In antiquity it was the largest city on the Appia between Capua and Tarentum, and from the sixth century on, it gave the Lombards their southern stronghold; it still is a large urban center, with a population more than twice the size of Venosa and Melfi combined. Unlike Melfi, ancient Beneventum had the stamp of ancient Rome impressed upon it in a big way: after the Samnites were defeated, a colony was established there in the third century BCE, and many reminders remain today. The Appia itself formed the *decumanus*, the main west-to-east road of any town laid out on the Roman plan, and its route through Benevento is roughly traced today by a major street, the Corso di Garibaldi. For a dozen blocks in the heart of the city the Corso is now an attractive pedestrian mall that is the scene of the *passeggiata*, the nightly ritual in which the citizens promenade up and down the street in small groups—on a Saturday, it seems, largely teenagers in all-male and all-female knots, eying each other, flirting, and behaving in a generally goofy way, with young couples or family groups interspersed.

This is not a scene exactly suggestive of antiquity (there would have been no promenading groups of teenagers, that's for sure), but there's still a family resemblance in the way that the street gives the townspeople a setting in which to see each other and be seen, in a performance of community that is a major social institution.

Then, too, literally a stone's throw off the Corso there stands the city's most conspicuous Roman monument, the wonderfully preserved Arch of Trajan, erected by "the Senate and people of Rome" in 114 CE at the end of the ancient city's main south-to-north street, the *cardo*. On each of the arch's two broad faces six friezes show the emperor in action: celebrating a triumph, dispensing land to veterans or food to children, promoting trade, meeting one or another god, or accepting the submission of Dacia (modern Transylvania) after one of his major military campaigns. In all of these panels the predominant mood conveyed—and surely the mood that was meant to be conveyed—is one of placid, effortless, even superhuman strength: here is a man on a par with the gods (not only does he meet gods, he is regularly portrayed as being of a stature greater than the other human beings around him), one who could perform acts with the most far-reaching consequences, the conquest of whole peoples, with no strain and no fuss. It is a mood utterly removed from that of the other great pictorial monument of his reign, the column in Trajan's Forum at Rome, which also commemorates the conquest of Dacia, but does so with a sequence of images that are unified by their ferocious violence. The arch in Benevento is the domesticated face of transcendent power, meant to soothe the citizenry and give them confidence. And because it was embedded in the town wall, as part of the city's fabric where the *cardo* ended and the new via Appia Traiana began, it became the face of Benevento that travelers saw first as they arrived and last as they departed.

So the sights and memories of Roman dominion are very much present in the city today. But there is another layer too, one that brings to mind—no, make that "brings to life"—Rome's ancient enemies, the Samnites, though the people have had no actual, earthly

Figure 21. Arch of Trajan, Benevento

existence for over two millennia. Another stone's throw off the
Corso, within sight of the arch and on the same south-to-north axis,
is the local university: not the Università degli Studi di Benevento,
but the Università degli Studi del Sannio—the University of Samnium. A little farther east on the Corso there is the archaeological museum, built onto the far side of the ninth-century church of
Santa Sofia and sharing its tranquil cloister: it is not the Museo di
Benevento but the Museo del Sannio—the Museum of Samnium.
And then there was the gentleman on the Ponte Leproso.

   As we were leaving Benevento to head toward Capua, we stopped
to examine the old bridge that allegedly takes its name from a leper
colony once quartered nearby. Its span of six arches carried the Appia
over the River Sábato as it entered the city from the southwest,
though some time has passed since it has had to bear any traffic. It is
as wide as the pieces of the ancient roadway found elsewhere, and a
series of smooth rectangular blocks runs like a dividing line down its

Figure 22. Arch of Trajan, Benevento

center, creating two lanes that are each wide enough for a cart. But grass and weeds sprout at the base of the sidewalls along its margins, and some of the cladding has fallen from the arches, exposing the old, flat brickwork beneath.

It was a Sunday morning, the Sábato rippled by audibly in the quiet, and only the occasional early walker passed as we poked about. After a bit, a man in his late seventies, possibly a bit older, approached to ask about our fascination with the bridge. I explained, to the limited extent I could, that we were interested in the via Appia and were tracing it through southern Italy. At that he launched into a spirited account, of what I was not sure, but clearly something that roused him to real passion. Shades of the inscription-interpreter outside Rome—save that now I was at even more of a loss, as the lack of a clear context and the speed with which he spoke left me simply snatching at sounds. I picked out the phrase "grande battaglia" and little else, beyond the fact that he seemed to be gesturing off to the southwest, the direction in which we were heading. A bit more, and the story stopped: shaking his raised fist, the man declared, "Benevento prima di Roma!"—"Benevento before Rome!," which is to say, "We're number one!"—then turned on his heel and walked smartly off down the center of the bridge, back into town.

Looking back, I give myself a pass by supposing that the early morning hour and my undercaffeinated state had just left me slow on the uptake. But slow I was, and puzzled. Great battle? What great battle? Assuming that the man had been referring to a great battle of World War II—he was certainly old enough to have lived through it and possibly old enough to have fought in it—I began to run through the possibilities in my mind. Salerno? No, that's almost due south from Benevento, not southwest. Anzio? No, that's west. Montecassino? No, northwest. I shook my head as we got into the car and headed off. Then about an hour later, as we drove through a mountain pass heading toward Capua, I glanced idly out my side window, saw a sign slip by, and felt the hair stand up on the back of my neck.

Figure 23. Ponte Leproso, Benevento

The sign I had seen read "Forche Caudine": the Caudine Forks. Of course! In 321 BCE, nine years before Appius Claudius began his road, a Roman army had marched through this same mountain pass near the start of the Second Samnite War, on its way from Capua to the enemy's territory. There was a safer if longer route along the coast, but the Roman generals, looking for a shortcut and relying on disinformation spread by Samnite soldiers posing as shepherds, chose the path through the mountains. When the army had advanced a good distance, it reached a point where the Samnites had blocked the way forward; by the time it turned to double back, the Samnites had come in from behind to seal the way out. So there the army sat, in a valley shadowed by steep mountains on both sides, as its food and water ran out and the Samnites pondered whether to let the soldiers go alive, and thereby earn the Romans' goodwill, or to kill them to the last man and thereby remove the Roman threat for generations.

In the end, the Samnites decided to do neither. Instead, every Roman would be stripped of his weapons and all else he carried save the single garment that he wore, and the entire army would be made to pass under a yoke (*iugum*) to signify its utter—and literal—subjugation before continuing on foot to Rome. This is how the historian Livy conjures up the Romans' intense shame as they anticipate the march:

> They pictured to themselves the enemy's yoke, the victors' mockery and arrogant glances, their unarmed passage between armed men on every side, and then the vile column's wretched progress through the cities of their allies, their return to fatherland and parents, where they themselves and their ancestors had often come in triumph. *They* alone had been beaten without wounds or weapons or a fight. *They* hadn't had the chance to draw their swords and close with the enemy. *They* had been given arms, strength, and courage—for nothing.

Then the march itself:

First the consuls were sent beneath the yoke, all but naked, then each officer met his shame in order of his rank, and then the legions, one by one. The enemy stood around under arms, reviling and mocking them, brandishing their swords, even wounding or killing some, if a glance more defiant than their disgrace warranted offended one of the victors. So they passed beneath the yoke and—what was almost harder to bear—before the eyes of their enemies, and emerged from the pass. Though they then seemed at last to see the light of day, as though they had been snatched from the realm of the dead, still the very light was grimmer to them than death in any form, as they looked upon their disgraced ranks.

The disaster at the Caudine Forks was by no means the worst military defeat that the Romans ever suffered, but it was certainly the most humiliating. And 2,300 years later, it still gave the gentleman on the Ponte Leproso reason to exult and gloat: "Benevento prima di Roma!"

The intensity of his pride and joy seemed so extraordinary, we suspected that we had just happened upon an elderly man with a particular passion for the past. So on a subsequent visit to Benevento we ran a modest test. At dinner one evening, we fell into conversation with the owner of the restaurant, a man in his late fifties or early sixties, and because the restaurant was near the Roman amphitheater and other excavations, the talk came around to Benevento's great age and its history. When I said, simply, "Forche Caudine?," the owner looked momentarily startled; then his face took on the most sublime expression of sly delight, as he brought his hands together in front of his chest, rocked them gently back and forth, and said, "Il topolino ha battuto il grande leone!"—"The mouse beat the great lion!"

Very well, we thought, perhaps it's a generational thing, a story that people of a certain age learned at school decades ago, but no more. So back at our hotel, after determining that the twenty-something clerk at the front desk was a native of Benevento, we asked her if she knew about the Forche Caudine. Of course, she said: "After all, I am a *Sannita.*" Hearing a modern young woman declare that she is a Samnite in the opening years of the twenty-first century—well, that really required some effort to get my mind around. Taken literally, as a declaration of ethnicity, it's of course complete nonsense, no matter what definition or criteria of ethnicity you want to apply: a citizen of Minnesota in the year 4000 might as well declare that he's a Swede. On the other hand, I suspect that come the year 4000 some citizens of Alabama and Mississippi will still prefer to call the Civil War "The War between the States," and something like that must have been a good part of what was going on in this case. As a declaration of local pride and allegiance, and maybe especially as a declaration of what one is *not*—*not* Roman, *not* part of the center—it packed a pretty fair wallop.

From Benevento the Appia threaded its way through mountain passes, first southwest through Montesarchio, then northwest toward Santa Maria Capua Vetere. But before it makes for Capua the modern road takes a more northerly tack, to pass first through Caserta—capital of the province of the same name and self-proclaimed buffalo mozzarella capital of the world—to the east. Whereas Caserta did not even exist in antiquity, old Capua was one of the great cities in Italy, at various times envied by the Romans for its luxury and feared as a possible rival. Unhappily for the Capuans, they sided with Hannibal in the Second Punic War (218–201 BCE) and were stripped of their autonomy when Rome took the city in 211.

Both Caserta and old Capua, it must be said, are pretty charmless places today. So is the plain, a dead ringer for Florida scrub, that the Appia crosses between Capua and Mondragone on the coast, a harsh landscape that encourages bleak thoughts. Traveling this stretch, I found my mind turning back to Capua, one of the places where the culture of gladiatorial games began, and its amphitheater—nearly as large as Rome's Colosseum, and much older—and from there quickly enough to Spartacus, whose uprising began at Capua in

73 BCE and scared Rome witless for the next two years. A later historian tells us that when the rebellion was put down, Marcus Crassus, Caecilia Metella's father-in-law, crucified the six thousand survivors among Spartacus's followers "along the whole length of the road from Capua to Rome." The ghastly math is easy. Six thousand crosses, one every 105 feet for 120 miles: a colleague suggests to his students that they picture the same carnage stretching from New York to Wilmington, Delaware, along I-95. I imagine the dying staked out over the plain to the sea, then following the contours of the coast north and west, through Minturno to Formia and beyond.

Formia to Rome, 82 miles

Fondi (Fundi)	12 miles
Terracina (Tarracina)	13 miles
"Ad Medias"	9 miles
"Forum Appii"	8 miles
"Tres Tabernae"	9 miles
Ariccia (Aricia)	16 miles
Frattocchie (Bovillae)	5 miles
Rome (Roma)	10 miles

There was still more reason to think of death when we reached Formia. Not that it's a grim or depressing place—far from it. It is now pretty much what it was in antiquity, a resort town that looks out on the Mediterranean and provides a place to relax in the sun. For wealthy Romans, it was one among many places along the coast that gave refuge from the heat and bustle of the capital, and many of them built villas here, down by the sea or up in the hills that rise quickly from the shore.

Today, however, the most conspicuous reminder of antiquity here is not a villa, but a tomb that tradition assigns to one of the greatest Romans of all. This is "Cicero's tomb"—though of course most of my brain knows that there's not the least chance it really is Cicero's. He died as an outlaw on the lam, and whatever postmortem attentions his body received would not have run to this monument, a towering drum set on a square base along the same lines as Caecilia Metella's. But still: the place—nearly within sight of the sea and right on what must have been the ancient Appia—is evocative if you know the story.

Marcus Tullius Cicero is unavoidable in my line of work, and not the sort of man who provokes mild emotions in those who make his acquaintance. Loathing and affection are the only choices. By now I have spent enough time in his company, through teaching and writing, to work past the first of those feelings and arrive at the second. Certainly, he is everything that those who loathe him say: an egotist who was impossibly high-maintenance as a friend; often blinkered and bloviating as a statesman; moody, inconstant, and self-dramatizing as a man; and—what finally did him in—not nearly as clever a political player as he thought he was, or as his enemies actually were. Yet he was also a loyal friend in his turn, and witty company, a man who (I think) really did try to do what he thought was right, and who along the way wrote some of the best prose ever composed in any language, with the same impact on the future of Latin that Shakespeare and the King James Version of the Bible have had on English. But above all he left himself exposed and accessible, and that is the thing in the end that moves me beyond simple respect.

A chief reason Cicero is so easy to loathe is that he left so much of himself on view. We know him better than we can know any human being in Western history before Saint Augustine, because no one in the West before Augustine left so large a written legacy of such a personal kind. The texts, and the body of commentary that has grown up around them, fill ten feet of shelving in my office, and my collection is not especially large: speeches, rhetorical treatises, philosophical tracts, and above all the correspondence, over twenty years' worth, that he carried on with family, friends, and enemies. Of course most of the writing is carefully calculated, intended to present the writer in the best possible light in whatever circumstance prompted the writ-

Figure 24. "Tomb of Cicero," Formia

ing: that is one of the jobs that rhetoric is supposed to do, and Cicero was a master of the craft. But even though the writing may not offer a transparent window on his soul, it does give excellent access to his lively mind. You see the wheels turning, you come to understand the move that's being made and anticipate the move that's coming next, and in so doing you reach across more than twenty centuries in a way that is exhilarating and moving.

But anticipating the move that's coming next is something that Cicero himself was only middling good at when it came to politics, and that brings us back to his tomb. Long story short: after Julius Caesar had emerged as victor from the civil wars of the early 40s BCE and accumulated powers that Cicero thought tyrannical, he rejoiced when Caesar was assassinated on the Ides of March in 44. Not only was the tyrant gone, but Cicero saw a chance to reestablish the sort of senatorial governance that he favored. So over the next twenty months he played a dangerous game, and he lost.

He calculated that he could use Caesar's grand-nephew and heir, Octavian—a boy of eighteen at the time of his uncle's death—to displace Caesar's political and military lieutenant, Mark Antony, and then get rid of Octavian when he had served his purpose: "the young man is to be praised," he wrote in a letter, "honored, and gotten out of the way." (He never could resist a good line, sometimes to his pain: this one did him no good when it got back to Octavian.) Cicero's calculation, however, failed to take the measure of the young man in question, who proved to be one of the most cunning and ruthless eighteen-year-olds the world has seen. So when Octavian and Antony came to an understanding and joined forces, Cicero had the ground cut out from under him. In November of 43 Octavian, Antony, and a third man, the aristocrat Marcus Lepidus, were voted absolute powers as "the three men to set the commonwealth on a sound footing"—the Triumvirate. And so for the second time in forty years Rome saw "proscriptions," publicly posted lists of men who had been declared outlaws: the men were to be hunted down and killed, their heads brought back to Rome and exchanged for a bounty, their property forfeited to the community. The names of Cicero, his brother, Quintus, and both their sons were on the lists.

Quickly, Cicero left Rome. What happened next made for a tale that historians liked to wring for all it was worth. Here's my favorite version, by Livy again:

> First he had fled to his estate in Tusculum, then by a cross-country route to the one in Formiae, since he intended to embark at Caieta [now Gaeta, a port about five miles away] and set off. He was carried out to sea several times, but at one moment the offshore winds carried him back, at another the ship's tossing in the impenetrable swell was more than he could bear. At length he was seized by revulsion for both flight and life and returned to his villa, which was little more than a mile from the sea. "I shall die," he said, "in the fatherland I have often saved." It is generally agreed that his slaves were prepared, gallantly and loyally, to fight to the end, but that he himself ordered them to set his sedan chair down and bear calmly what an unjust fortune forced upon them. As he leaned out and offered his neck, unflinchingly, his head was cut off—nor was that enough for the soldiers' brutish cruelty: they cut off his hands, too, reviling them for having written what they had against Antony [i.e., the hostile *Philippics*]. The head was brought back to Antony and at his order placed between the two hands on the Rostra where he had often been heard, as consul, as ex-consul, and in that very year speaking against Antony, his eloquence received with wonder such as no human voice has ever enjoyed. His fellow citizens could scarcely lift their eyes, brimming with tears, to look at the hacked limbs.

It was December 7, 43 BCE; what happened to the rest of his body is not recorded, but it is unlikely to have been worthy of the man. The only male of the family to survive was his good-for-nothing son, a wastrel and wine-sack also named Marcus, who had the good luck to be "studying" in Athens when hell broke loose at home. Standing by the tomb and recalling Cicero's head falling to the Appia, I found it hard to suppress the thought that if a Marcus Cicero had to be murdered that day, the wrong one had been found.

If Cicero's failed dash for safety brought him overland to Formia, as Livy says (accounts do differ), he passed over the stretch of the Appia that turns inland at Terracina and follows an arc through Fondi and the Monti Aurunci before it descends to Formia by the sea. The road took this detour, rather than following the coastline where the rich kept their seaside villas, because of the position of Terracina, where the promontory that met the sea prevented a road from passing: it was not until the reign of Trajan, more than four hundred years after the road was first built, that a way was cut, down through over 110 feet of rock, to clear a passage. As you came from the south, then, Terracina had to be approached from the inland side, through the last rugged terrain of the journey.

It's in the Monti Aurunci that the most extensive stretch of the Appia outside Rome has been reclaimed, about a mile and a half of road embraced by what is now a *parco naturale*. It's a marvelous setting and a wonderful place for a hike, completely isolated except for the occasional hiss of an auto on the modern road that runs nearby, parallel to the ancient. Stands of citrus trees at its base give way to whatever wild growth can cling to the rocky hills that loom on the right of the road as you climb and then, after briefly continuing their descent below the road, rise up again on the left. On a hot afternoon in late spring a welcome breeze drifts through the valley, and up ahead a small red fox trots across the road and into the brush. There are baffles at both ends of the trail to keep motor vehicles out, but abundant patties make it plain that cows are frequent visitors— unless (a possibility, to judge from the size) these are the relics of Hannibal's elephants. The grade becomes steeper as you climb, and lines of raised stone cross the road every ten yards or so like speed bumps, perhaps once intended to slow runaway wagons.

About a third of the way up the trail, a series of five terraces rises from the roadway to support what was once a temple of Apollo on the hillside, and it was here that Laura and I had our only serious

Figure 25. Via Appia, Parco Naturale dei Monti Aurunci

aesthetic disagreement of the trip. Her position held that the builders, had they been serious about it, would not have plunked the temple down on the side of the hill but would have built it all the way on top, like the great temple of Jupiter Anxur, seven hundred feet above the sea at Terracina, or the shrines of Machu Picchu. Those are places, she said, that make you understand why people thought them holy: this was just a lazy job. On my view, this was an unreasonable comparison. Whereas Jupiter Anxur would have been visible for miles out to sea, no one would have seen this temple had it been placed on the hilltop: where it stood, it would be have been visible to every traveler coming up the road, in fact would have been the center of attention, its gleaming marble set off against the green background of the mountain woods.

Whatever the aesthetic pros and cons might be, however, a climb up the terraces makes plain how useful the temple's site was for another purpose it came to serve; and this brings us to another bit of layering in which the Appia is involved, in a new era. As you walk along the roadway here, it becomes clear almost immediately that it's not all of a piece: segments of the ancient, rounded basalt paving stones alternate with segments where the paving is strictly rectangular and cut from different stone. This was the work of the Bourbons, who came to control the Kingdom of Naples in 1735 and put significant work into maintaining the road. They also made significant use of the temple, which had long since been converted to serve as a fort or, at times, a bandit lair. Set halfway up the hill, it's high enough to command a view of the entire valley, down to the Plain of Fondi and beyond to the Monti Ausoni, and close enough to the road to make it possible to launch quick strikes.

As the fort of Sant' Andrea it is particularly remembered for two incidents that bring us to the brink of a unified Italy. Under the Bourbons, the brigand-turned-soldier-turned-legend Michael Pezza, better known as Fra Diavolo, used the site late in 1798 to stage raids on the advancing French Revolutionary forces to prevent them from advancing through the pass against the Kingdom of Naples. The

Figure 26. From the temple of Apollo (fort of Sant' Andrea), Parco Naturale dei Monti Aurunci

French were soon successful by other means, but Pezza's exploits are remembered on a plaque at the site: "To Michael Pezza, 1771–1806. In memory of Fra Diavolo, the man who in December 1798 . . . blocked the advance of the Franco-Polish army in the gorge of Sant' Andrea with energetic, courageous, and indomitable resistance." Two generations later, in the autumn of 1860, after the Kingdom of Naples had merged with the Kingdom of Sicily to form the Kingdom of the Two Sicilies (1816), the fort became a site of battle for the final time, when Francis II, the last king of the Two Sicilies, attempted to stop the advance of the Piedmontese army. The king had by then withdrawn from Naples and barricaded himself in Gaeta, the same port from which Cicero had tried to make his escape. After the Piedmontese advance could not be stopped, Francis II surrendered in February 1861 and left for exile in Austria. The following month, Victor Emmanuel II, King of Sardinia, became the first monarch of the united Kingdom of Italy.

Continuing Rome-ward from the Monti Aurunci, you needed a morning to cross the Plain of Fondi to get back to Terracina on the coast. Then for the first nineteen miles out of Terracina, heading northwest toward Rome, you had the option of traveling by barge along the canal, the Decennovium, that ran alongside the road. But the canal and the road passed through the malarial Pomptine Marshes, an uninhabitable waste whose presence ensured that there would be no substantial settlements in the forty-odd miles between Terracina and the hill town of Ariccia.

Human habitation in this region mostly clung to the hills set back from the sea, high above the marshes. Attempts to drain the marshes were planned many times, and some attempts were actually made; in his diary Goethe described one of them in optimistic terms:

> From one cross-journey, one cannot, of course, really judge such a vast and ambitious project as the drainage operations that have been undertaken at the orders of the Pope [Pius VI], but it looks to me as though they are going to be largely successful. Imagine a wide valley running from north to south with hardly any fall, but dipping towards the mountains in the east and rising towards the sea in the west. Down its whole length runs the straight line of the restored Via Appia, flanked on its right [Goethe is heading south] by the main canal which drains all the land on the seaward side, so that this now has been reclaimed for agriculture. . . . The land on the mountain side presents a more difficult problem. Cross-channels emptying into the main canal have been dug through the embankment of the road, but these cannot drain off the water. I am told there is a plan for digging a second drainage canal along the base of the mountains.

But the plans came to nothing, and all attempts to drain the marshes failed until the Fascists at last succeeded in turning this part of Lazio into the fertile plain that we see today, set against the backdrop of the Monti Lepini.

Figure 27. Pomptine Plain and Monti Lepini

It took ancient travelers a full day's journey to put the marshes behind them and begin the climb into the clear air of the Alban Hills,
where the volcanic lakes Nemi and Albano still offer refreshment to
Romans seeking relief from the city's heat: here the pope's summer
residence in Castel Gandolfo looks across Lago Albano toward the
heights where the Romans offered sacrifice each year to "Jupiter of
Latium." From the hills it would be a half day's walk back to the
walls of the capital. As for us on our four wheels, we could virtually
coast the rest of the way, down into the plain of Rome's suburbs, to
the point near the prostitutes of the ninth milestone, where we had
stopped our outbound hike and turned back to meet the misdirected
but resolute trekkers from Houston.

EPILOGUE

Mullet in Tusculum

So we had finished our travels on the Appian Way. Tomorrow we would surrender the rental car, minus a driver-side rearview mirror, thanks to another tight squeeze (some people never learn). Now we were at our hotel, a converted villa in the hills of Grottaferrata just east of Rome, watching from the terrace at dusk as the city's lights stretched out toward the sea and shimmered in the haze left by the day's heat: pretty perfect. After enjoying the cool evening air a bit longer, we went in to dinner at the hotel's restaurant, where we talked about our trip and the shape of this book, and made our choices from the menu, the mullet for me. It wasn't until the main course was served, and the fish was put before me, that I realized what I had done, and began to laugh.

I should explain.

I had instantly liked the idea of spending our last night in this spot, poised between the cool hills of Tusculum, the site of Cicero's favorite villa, two miles to the northeast, and Fratocchie (ancient Bovillae) in Rome's suburbs, three miles to the southwest, where one of Cicero's great enemies, Publius Clodius Pulcher—"Little Pretty Boy" (Pulchellus), as Cicero liked to call him—was murdered on the Appian Way in 52 BCE. Clodius, now there was a piece of work: a member of the same patrician clan as Appius Claudius (the names "Clodius" and "Claudius" are the same, despite the different spellings), an instigator of mutinies, a demagogue, a louche reprobate, and utterly vindictive. Ten years earlier, disguised as a woman, he had been caught stealing into a solemn religious celebration forbidden to men, so that he could keep an appointment with his lover of the moment: the woman happened to be Caesar's wife, the celebration happened to be held in Caesar's house, and the result of Clodius's discovery was a religious and political scandal of the first order. In the trial for sacrilege that followed, Clodius contended that he had been elsewhere in Italy that day, but when Cicero was called as a witness, he exploded the alibi. Clodius was acquitted nonetheless, thanks to spectacular bribery, and from that time relations between the two men were in a state of *inimicitiae*, or feud. Cicero, for his part, was soon publicly bantering that Clodius slept with one or more of his own sisters, an insult so far over the line by Roman standards that you would offer it only to a man you would gladly see dead. Clodius, for his part, maneuvered politically until he reached a position from which he could inflict on Cicero one of the great disasters of his life, the exile that drove him from Rome in March of 58.

While Cicero was away, first in northern Greece and then on the coast of what is today Albania, his friends and supporters back in Rome worked for his recall, until they succeeded in August of 57. One of his benefactors was Titus Annius Milo, a minor politician and major thug who contributed significantly to the violent turn that Roman political life took as things spun out of control in the 50s. The dominant political alliance of Caesar, Pompey, and Crassus, which had kept the lid on trouble in the first half of the decade, began to crack and—after Crassus died at the Parthians' hands in 53—crumbled. The city's institutions, which had sustained nearly five centuries of republican government, were now in a state of collapse that could not be denied, as the rivalry between Caesar and Pompey edged toward direct confrontation, then exploded in the civil wars that began in January 49. But three years earlier, Milo had been involved in a violent confrontation of his own.

On January 18 in the year 52, Milo was traveling on the Appia from Rome to his hometown in southeast Latium, seated in a cart with his wife and surrounded by a substantial entourage, many of whom were armed. As he reached Bovillae, Clodius approached from the opposite direction with an armed entourage of his own. There was a long history between the two men, including plenty of violence—Clodius had on more than one occasion attacked Milo's house in the city—but on this particular day they passed each other without incident. Or nearly so: though the two principals ignored each other, words were exchanged between their followers, then shoves, until fighting broke out, and when Clodius fled, wounded, into a nearby tavern, Milo ordered him to be dragged out onto the Appia and killed. Rioting followed: Clodius's corpse was brought to the Forum in Rome, where the next day his followers burned the body in the senate house, and then burned the senate house itself. Milo was soon brought to trial, not for murder but for the political crime of *vis:* seditious violence, actions taken by force that threatened the community as a whole.

When Milo's trial began in April, Cicero defended him, repaying the favors that Milo had done him while he was in exile. But when Cicero rose to speak, it was clear that this was not going to be his day. His delivery was hesitant in the face of the clamor from Clodius's supporters (trials were held outdoors in the Forum), the speech was weak, and it was obvious as soon as he finished that he had failed. Anticipating conviction, which would have brought exile and the confiscation of his property, Milo went into voluntary exile before the trial was finished, thereby salvaging his estate. He chose Marseilles, a destination popular with Romans in Milo's circumstances: founded as a Greek colony six centuries earlier, it was a place of real culture where one could live very comfortably. Cicero, deeply unhappy with his speech, later reworked it, and it is the revised version, an exercise in *esprit d'escalier*, that we have today. When Cicero sent Milo a copy, he replied gracefully (or sarcastically) that he was glad Cicero had not delivered so splendid a speech at his trial. The reason: it would have deprived him of the chance to enjoy the excellent local mullet.

The past, she is everywhere, in layer upon layer, before our eyes and beneath our feet. In Italy, and on the Appian Way, there are more layers than in most places, deeper, richer, and more complex. Sometimes, to find them, you need to ask a lucky question, or have a chance meeting, or stumble into a foolish accident. Sometimes they're no farther away than the dinner plate under your nose.

ADVICE·FOR·THE·TRAVELER

There are countless guides available, in print and online, for anyone planning travel to, in, and around Rome, and resources for traveling in the south, though skimpier, are not hard to come by (type "Basilicata Italy travel" into Google, and you'll get about 600,000 results). This is not the place for that sort of advice, though I do have one practical suggestion for the southern leg of the trip: use a travel agent who specializes in Italy, for it will save you many headaches and much hassle, at a cost that is truly negligible relative to the overall expense (we used Connoisseur's Travel, an excellent agency based in Chicago). That general suggestion aside, the notes that follow concentrate on the experience of the via Appia itself.

READING

Excellent preparation for traveling the Appia can be found in *The Appian Way: From Its Foundation to the Middle Ages*, a sumptuous production edited by Ivana Della Portella and published by Oxford University Press for the Getty Museum. It is by far the best of the very few books in English that treat the whole length of the road for a general audience, with a marvelous collection of photographs and a series of essays on the successive segments of the route. The essays are informative, if impersonal and a bit stiff, and though the book is not intended to be a field guide—other considerations aside, its hardcover, 8.5″× 10.5″ format makes it a bit unwieldy for that sort of use—each essay contains an "itinerary" that can be photocopied and carried for reference.

The two best English-language guides to the archaeological sites in and around the capital are *Rome*, also from Oxford University Press, in a second edition (2010) by Amanda Claridge, Judith Toms, and Tony Cubberley; and *Rome and Environs: An Archaeological Guide*, by Filippo Coarelli (Berkeley, 2008). Both are available in paperback, and both are helpful in an "on your left you will see . . . , and then on your right . . ." sort of way. For the Appia specifically, the itineraries available online—gratis and in English—at the archeological park's website are well worth having on hand as you walk (http://www.parcoappiaantica.it/en/default.asp). In Italian there are two sets of itineraries that cover the length of the Appia, one produced by Lorenzo Quilici—the greatest modern scholar of the road—for the series *Itinerari d'arte e di cultura / Via Appia*; the other by a range of authors for the series *Antiche strade*.

A bit further afield, Ray Laurence's *Roads of Roman Italy: Mobility and Cultural Change* (London, 1999), while unmistakably an academic book, gives an accessible and imaginative overview of its subject. In a different vein entirely, there's Steven Saylor's *Murder on the Appian Way* (New York, 1997), about the death of Clodius, one of a series of mystery-thrillers featuring "Gordianus the Finder" that take episodes in Cicero's career as their starting points: written with a scholar's sense of the period and a novelist's feel for character, the whole series has given me many hours of pleasure.

Then there are two books written from a personal point of view and in a personal voice. In *Between Two Seas: A Walk Down the Appian Way* (London, 1991), Charles Lister, a former BBC announcer and schoolmaster, offers a quirky account of a trek he made from Rome to Brindisi in 1961: though it has interesting reflections on what a still very rural southern Italy was like fifty years ago, the writing is often dire—if the Mezzogiorno in the middle third of the twentieth century is what you're after, far better to read Carlo Levi's masterpiece, *Christ Stopped at Eboli*. Peter Stothard's *On the Spartacus Road* (New York, 2010), as its title suggests, is not about the Appia itself, though the trail of Spartacus's insurrection inevitably overlaps with the Appia for significant stretches: as literate and engaging as you would expect a book by the editor of the *Times Literary Supplement* to be, it does not bear much love for the Romans. (Whereas earlier generations of British scholars and intellectuals tended to admire the Roman Empire as a forerunner of their own, the consensus in postimperial Britain has shifted, and there now seems to be broad agreement that the Romans were bastards. My view is that the Romans were what they were, and that understanding what they were does not advance by taking an attitude toward them, especially when the attitude is one of moral superiority.) Finally, if some background reading would be useful, to help you tell the Angevins from the Aragonese (and from all the rest who seized, held, and lost chunks of southern Italy over the centuries), I can recommend Christopher Duggan's *A Concise History of Italy* (Cambridge, 1994).

WALKING

It will already be clear, from the beginning of this book, that I emphatically do not recommend walking the first two miles of the Appia beyond the porta San Sebastiano: between the traffic and the encroachment that has privatized most of the antiquities worth seeing, the risk is not remotely offset by the gain. For that matter—as I discovered only afterward—the archaeological park itself advises against walking on the particularly terrifying stretch between the entry to the catacombs of San Callisto and the catacombs of San Sebastiano. Instead, it is suggested that pedestrians follow the driveway that leads from the entry to San Callisto's grounds to the catacombs proper themselves, running parallel to the Appia. This is a sensible alternative, especially if you intend to take the tour. If you simply must walk on that stretch of the Appia, do it on a Sunday, when the road is supposed to be closed to vehicles and the police make a reasonable attempt to enforce the ban.

There are three alternatives to walking those initial miles. First, and most expensive, you can take a taxi to, for example, the catacombs (except on Sunday). Archeobus provides another alternative, a system of open buses that circulate on a fixed route linking noteworthy ancient sites throughout Rome, including a couple of stops on the Appia: once you have your ticket, you can hop on and off ad lib all day—though if the Appia is your only goal, and you do not plan to hop on and off all day elsewhere in the city, this too is an expensive alternative.

The option I prefer entails an easy combination of Metro and bus (one low fare allows you to ride both): either the Metro B line to the Circo Massimo, followed by a #118 bus to a stop at the San Sebastiano catacombs, from which you can continue outbound safely on foot; or the Metro A line to Colli Albani, followed by a #660 bus to the Cecilia Metella stop, from which you can continue out or take a short walk back toward the catacombs.

Travelers for whom the word "park" suggests the state and national park systems of the United States, which offer various amenities for visitors should know that there are no comparable amenities in the archaeological park of the via Appia antica. Between the San Sebastiano and Cecilia Metella bus stops there are several private establishments—one very bad restaurant (on the right as you walk away from the city), one very good restaurant (L'Archeologia, on the left), and a small café at Cecilia Metella where bicycles can also be rented. But between Cecilia Metella and the tomb of Gallienus six Roman miles away, there are no facilities of any sort, beyond a small bar and restaurant attached to a tennis club on the via degli Eugenii, off the Appia about a mile and a half beyond Cecilia Metella. (A sign on the Appia says that the club is 100 meters away, a bold lie: it's 600 meters.) If you plan to spend a day in the best part of the park, walking out from Cecilia Metella, see to the needs of nature before you start and pack a lunch with plenty of water.

South of Rome you will do more driving than walking, but of course there are a number of places you will want to explore on foot. Here is a baker's dozen of must-stops, with their coordinates in parentheses so you can pinpoint them on Google Maps or "fly" to them on Google Earth.

> Terracina: here the Appia grazes a "purgatory church" and the remains of the Roman Capitolium before entering the ancient forum (the central municipal plaza of today's city), where it passes the cathedral of San Cesareo, which occupies the site of a temple of Rome and Augustus (41°17′30.64″N 13°14′55.77″E); high above the town, the ruins of the temple of Jupiter Anxur look out over the sea (41°17′26.73″N 13°15′34.38″E).
>
> Parco Naturale dei Monti Aurunci, between Fondi and Itri (41°18′46.27″N 13°29′16.72″E).
>
> Cicero's tomb, Formia (41°15′05.61″N 13°34′42.99″E).
>
> Ancient Minturnae (41°14′59.30″N 13°44′05.69″E).
>
> The amphitheater, Santa Maria Capua Vetere (41°05′09.25″N 14°15′00.33″E).
>
> Trajan's Arch, Benevento (41°07′56.89″N 14°46′44.86″E).
>
> Ancient Aeclanum (41°03′16.4″N 15°00′36.20″E).
>
> Melfi Castle (40°59′54.18″N 15°39′10.33″E).
>
> Ancient Venusia and the church of the Santissima Trinità, Venosa (40°58′08.14″N 15°49′38.82″E).
>
> Gravina: The cathedral and the churches of Santa Maria del Suffragio and Saint Basil are all within a short walk of one another (40°49′06.41″N 16°24′49.39″E). Not on the Appia but worth a brief detour is the city of Altamura, nine miles away, which has a distinguished cathedral begun by Frederick II of Swabia and bread that is famous throughout Italy (40°49′38.88″N 16°33′11.34″E).
>
> The archaeological museum, Taranto (40°28′23.26″N 17°14′21.42″E).
>
> Oria (40°29′54.27″N 17°38′32.13″E).
>
> The harbor, Brindisi: The cathedral and the archaeological museum are also nearby, about a hundred yards from the waterfront (40°38′28.35″N 17°56′47.55″E).

DRIVING

Cycling from Rome to Brindisi is an option, one taken up not long ago by a graduate student in my department and her husband, who made the trip in twelve days. But that route is for people younger, fitter, and bolder than we are, and I assume that most readers who are tempted to make the trip will have the same point of view. If you've driven in Italy before, you know that it is not terribly challenging (even in Rome—honestly); if you haven't, the following bullet points might be of some use:

- Rent a car no larger than you absolutely require for yourself, any companions, and your luggage. We drove the Appia twice, the first time in a car that was too large, the second in one that was just right, and both scrapes in which we were involved on the first tour were largely attributable to the size of the auto (largely, but not entirely: see below).
- Italian drivers are on average more aggressive than drivers in the United States (save in Massachusetts), and it is not for nothing that most traffic signals have a red light that is twice the diameter of the green. That said, their aggression rarely translates into real risk: they will, for example, seize on the slightest opening (sometimes, even, an imagined opening) to merge with a line of traffic, but I cannot recall a single instance of the high-speed tailgating that is common on American roads. (Perhaps the self-regard that causes an Italian driver to thrust himself ahead in line serves also to apply the brakes of self-preservation.) The rate of traffic fatalities in Italy, per 100,000 miles traveled, is significantly lower than it is in the United States.
- You should acquire an International Driver's Permit (IDP). Though you will probably have no need to use it (rental agencies certainly showed no interest in mine), the one occasion on which I did produce it was the exception that proved the rule and justified every one of the fifteen dollars it had cost. While driving just

south of Minturno, I was waved over by a Guardia di Finanza officer, who (I believe) had been alerted by radio from a patrol car that had spotted me passing in a no-passing zone. (What was that about? It's a national sport!) But after determining that Italian was not my native language and looking over the IDP, the officer handed it back to me with a "Bene, grazie," and waved us on our way.

Finally, if you have a GPS, either leave it at home or strictly limit yourself to using it to find a specific address (say, of a hotel) on entering one of the larger towns. Beyond that use, the only difficulties the device helped us out of were those it had led us into in the first place. There were two key problems. First, in a region where the quality of state and provincial roads can vary dramatically, the mapping software was insufficiently attentive to the character of the surface onto which it directed us, as one anecdote from our experience on the via Appia Traiana will illustrate. After being told by the robotic voice to "turn onto the unpaved roadway" for perhaps the sixth time in an afternoon, I brightened on seeing the name of the town we were trying to reach written on the roadblock meant to keep us off the road onto which we had just been sent; for her part, Laura didn't so much brighten on seeing the roadblock as turn white. "Actually," I chirped, about a half mile later, "this has to give us a *much* better idea of what travel was like in antiquity than *anything* we've done in the past few days"; this observation was greeted by a certain amount of hysterical laughter. But when a few minutes later I nearly burned out the clutch after stalling on a steep grade behind a tractor, I turned tail and fled, then wasted much of the afternoon trying to recover a drivable surface. Second, the software is understandably incapable of gauging the relation between a given vehicle's size and the width of the street on which it is traveling, and streets in the historical centers of Italian towns, also understandably, were not built with the dimensions of modern vehicles in mind: hence our two scrapes. For the most part, the road system in southern

Italy is not crowded with a confusing array of options, and you will do much better to use a set of decent road maps.

MAPS

The best maps for tracing the ancient route of the Appia—as for locating any other feature of the ancient Mediterranean basin and its environs—are found in the *Barrington Atlas of the Greek and Roman World* (Princeton, 2000), one of the great recent achievements in ancient studies: the maps of central and southern Italy (maps 44 and 45, respectively) are well worth photocopying and carrying with you. The distinguished editor of the *Barrington Atlas*, Richard Talbert, has more recently written a book on the *Tabula Peutingeriana—Rome's World: The Peutinger Map Reconsidered* (Cambridge, 2010)—and you can view the entire *Tabula* as a seamless whole, in color, on the website that supplements the book (select Map A at http://www .cambridge.org/us/talbert/).

For the modern road system, the Michelin maps for "Italie Centre" and "Italie Sud" are reasonably priced and certainly adequate, but I recommend instead (or in addition) the series of maps dedicated to Italy's administrative provinces, from Lazio to Brindisi, which can be purchased easily online (just type "road maps Italy provinces" into Google, and you'll find a vendor within a few clicks). These are easier to handle than the rather unwieldy Michelin maps and, more important, they're drawn on a larger scale (1:250,000 vs. 1:400,000); the added detail is worth the expense. Note, in any case, that whereas any map you use will identify the roads you take by number (for example, SS7 = *Strada statale* 7), the signage on the ground rarely uses the number to identify a road or to indicate a choice between roads. Instead, signs use the names of towns, typically pointing you toward the next town located on a given road. In using a map, then, you need to look one move ahead, having in mind both where you are and the name of the next town in the direction you want to go.

EXCHANGES

I've already sung the praises of the people we met, for their kindness and goodwill, and I'll do some more of that soon, but first I should note a regional peculiarity that you will encounter every day, one that I found puzzling and annoying, if finally a bit endearing. It concerns the interaction of people and euro notes. If you offer to pay a $12 tab with a $20 bill in a shop or eating place in the States, it will be taken as an obvious thing to do; in fact, if you try to pay a $2 tab with a $20 bill, you will be met by nothing more than the occasional, "Got anything smaller?" But try to pay a €12 tab with a €20 note in any establishment in southern Italy: looks of hurt and reproach as employees empty their own pockets in search of change, then perhaps a dash to the shop next door. As for €50 or €100 notes: please, be serious. One evening in Benevento, when I tried to pay for our €40-odd worth of dinner with a €100 note, the grandmotherly owner, with whom we'd been chatting on and off throughout the meal, recoiled and raised her hands in a defensive gesture, as though I'd drawn a weapon. But when we'd settled up and I put down the €5 note that is the conventional token of thanks for service above and beyond the cover charge, she quickly scooped it up and added it to a sheaf of notes, two inches thick, that she produced from her apron pocket. It was then that I decided, well, something's happening here, what it is ain't exactly clear . . . Whatever the cause of this quirk, I mention it on the chance that doing so will save you from spending an outsized chunk of a morning as I did, waiting on line in a bank to get change for some larger denomination notes. When you buy your euros, insist on nothing larger than €20 bills.

Currency is a medium of exchange and so a form of language, complete with its inevitable opacities and mistaken signals. Even more obviously, language is a form of language. I've already had more than one occasion to refer to my very imperfect grasp of Italian, but what I've left mostly unremarked is the openhearted willingness of people to work with me in my struggles. It is a cliché to speak of the kindness of the Italian people, and another to say that if you make an effort, people will cut you a generous amount of slack; but clichés are often clichés because they are true. Though English is less commonly spoken in the south than in Rome and farther north, you will generally find enough in hotels and restaurants to get by— but you should also try to meet people halfway. If you know no Italian, take along a simple phrasebook: I assure you that you will not only manage but take pleasure in the interchanges besides. Every exchange that we had—if we set aside a few taxi drivers in and around Rome who were actual thieves—added to our enjoyment and, yes, confirmed the clichés. Typical of these exchanges was our encounter with a young mother in Mirabella Eclano, whom we approached for directions after driving in circles for an hour looking for the site of ancient Aeclanum. She knew no English whatever, and she quickly gauged the limits of my Italian, but she shrugged, clapped her hands, and said, "Proviamo"—"Let's try." It came to nothing (we spent another hour driving in circles before stumbling on the site by chance), but that single verb remains one of my favorite memories of our travels.